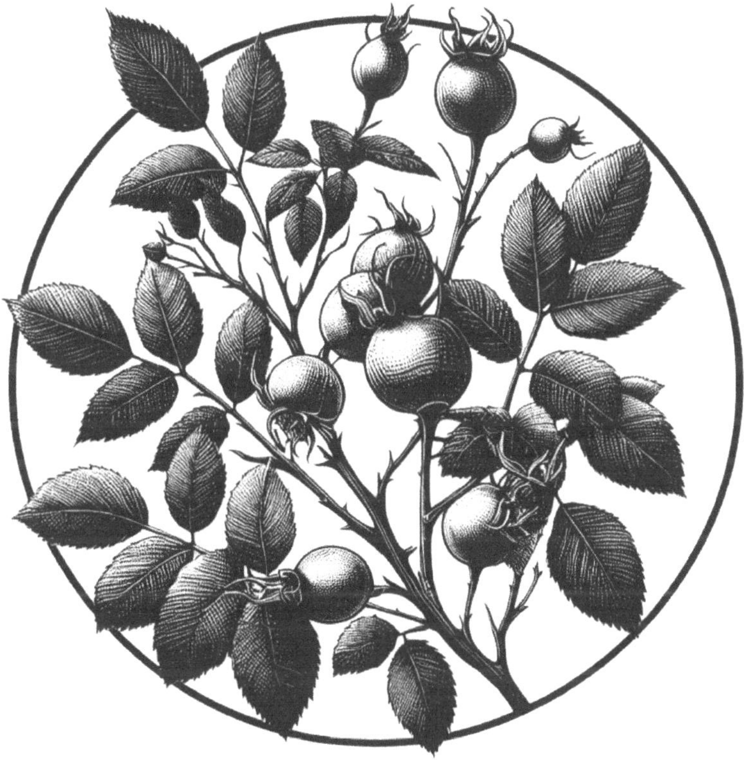

"The Rosehip Companion: Beverages" is a comprehensive guide that delves into the intricate world of rosehips and their multifaceted applications in the realm of beverages. This volume serves as a definitive resource for enthusiasts and professionals alike, offering a rich exploration of the diverse possibilities that arise from the integration of rosehips into a wide array of drinks, vinegars, cocktails, mocktails, and shrubs.

Readers are invited on a sensory journey as they discover the historical significance and cultural reverence attached to rosehips, gaining a deep understanding of their botanical intricacies and the nuances of their flavors. The volume delves into the art of crafting exquisite beverages, providing detailed insights into the cultivation, harvesting, and processing of these vibrant fruits, alongside a meticulous examination of the nutritional benefits they offer.

Through a meticulously curated collection of recipes, including ancient elixirs and contemporary libations, readers will be inspired to embark on an experiential exploration of the enchanting world of rosehip-based beverages. From revitalizing teas to elaborate cocktails infused with molecular gastronomy techniques, this volume offers a diverse and innovative assortment of creations that highlight the versatility and allure of rosehips.

Furthermore, the volume places a special emphasis on the art of crafting artisanal rosehip vinegars and shrubs, guiding readers through the intricate process of creating these complex yet harmonious concoctions. With a strong focus on techniques and mixology principles, readers will learn how to infuse these vinegars and shrubs into a plethora of contemporary and traditional beverages, elevating their drinking experiences with each carefully crafted sip.

"The Rosehip Companion: Beverages" sets the stage for an immersive and enlightening journey into the world of rosehips, offering readers a profound appreciation for the rich history, culinary applications, and sensorial pleasures derived from these captivating fruits and their derived products. This volume is an indispensable addition to the library of any beverage aficionado, mixologist, or culinary enthusiast seeking to explore the vibrant and enchanting realm of rosehip-based drinks and concoctions.

Rose Hips

The roses of the summer are all gone,
The roses of the summer are all gone;
But in the autumn woods are wild hips on.
There's a cheering, shining red in the thickets.
And the pickerel-weed is red by the brook.

-Mary E. Wilkins Freeman

The Rosehip Companion Volume 1: Beverages

ISBN Paperback: 978-1-989647-27-1

A Byrd Press Publication
Toronto
www.byrdpress.com
publisher@byrdpress.com

cover design R.H. Mason

Table of Contents

Part I: Introduction to Rosehips

Part II: Rosehips for the Mixologist

Drinks

Vinegars

What Are Rosehips?

The world of botanical treasures is vast, encompassing a plethora of plants with diverse uses and benefits. One such often overlooked yet invaluable component is the rosehip. These small, vibrant fruits, borne from the wild rose plant, carry within them a wealth of nutritional, medicinal, and cultural significance. Delving into the importance of understanding rosehips unveils their multifaceted contributions to human health, culinary arts, and ecological balance.

Nutritional and Medicinal Benefits
Rosehips, known for their high vitamin C content and rich antioxidant properties, play a vital role in promoting human well-being. Research has demonstrated their efficacy in boosting immune function, aiding in digestion, and supporting skin health. Understanding their nutritional composition sheds light on their potential to combat various ailments, thereby underscoring their significance in holistic wellness practices.

Culinary and Cultural Applications
Beyond their health benefits, rosehips have been an integral part of culinary traditions across diverse cultures. From flavorful jams and teas to delectable desserts, the incorporation of rosehips in culinary practices adds a unique and enriching dimension to gastronomy. Additionally, exploring their cultural significance unveils their role in folklore, art, and symbolism, making them an indispensable part of the cultural tapestry.

Environmental Sustainability and Conservation
The understanding of rosehips extends beyond their human-centric applications to encompass their ecological significance. The wild rose plants, from which rosehips are derived, contribute to biodiversity and ecological balance. Comprehending their role in sustaining local ecosystems highlights the need for responsible harvesting practices and conservation efforts to ensure their preservation for generations to come.

Economic and Commercial Viability
The economic viability of rosehips lies in their extensive use in various industries, including pharmaceuticals, cosmetics, and culinary markets. Their demand as a source of natural ingredients for skincare products, herbal supplements, and gourmet delicacies underscores the economic potential that can be harnessed through sustainable cultivation and commercialization. Recognizing their commercial value emphasizes the need for responsible management practices to balance economic gains with environmental sustainability.

Future Prospects and Research Endeavors
As research in the field of botany and natural remedies advances, the potential

of rosehips continues to unfold. Current research initiatives exploring their role in disease prevention, alternative medicine, and sustainable agriculture signal a promising future for these unassuming fruits. Understanding their evolving significance in the context of contemporary scientific developments underscores the need for continued exploration and research.

The significance of understanding rosehips transcends mere recognition of their physical attributes; it delves into their holistic contribution to human health, cultural heritage, environmental sustainability, and economic prosperity. Recognizing the multifaceted importance of rosehips inspires a collective responsibility to preserve their rich legacy and harness their potential for the betterment of both humanity and the natural world.

Rosehips: A Brief Historical Narrative

In the intricate tapestry of botanical history, the humble rosehip holds a significant place, symbolizing resilience, nourishment, and cultural heritage. Spanning centuries, the journey of the rosehip unfolds as a tale of human ingenuity, survival, and the interwoven relationship between nature and civilization.

Ancient Roots and Folklore
The earliest traces of the rosehip's significance can be found in the annals of ancient civilizations, where it was revered for its medicinal properties and revered as a symbol of vitality and protection. From the healing elixirs of traditional medicine to the captivating folk tales that speak of its mystical powers, the rosehip has long been entwined with human narratives of health, beauty, and enchantment.

Medieval Gardens and Royal Connotations
The medieval era witnessed the deliberate cultivation of rose plants, including those bearing the precious rosehips, within the lavish gardens of royalty and nobility. As a symbol of luxury and opulence, the rosehip became associated with wealth and sophistication, adorning the estates of monarchs and aristocrats, while also finding its way into the culinary delights of the elite, thereby cementing its place in the culinary heritage of the era.

Exploration and Global Spread
The Age of Exploration marked a pivotal chapter in the history of the rosehip, as seafaring expeditions carried this botanical treasure across continents, introducing it to new lands and cultures. Its resilience and adaptability allowed it to flourish in various climates, leading to its integration into diverse culinary and medicinal traditions worldwide. This global dissemination not only enriched local cuisines but also contributed to the exchange of knowledge and practices, fostering a global understanding of its value.

World Wars and Medicinal Revival

The tumultuous period of the World Wars brought the rosehip back to the forefront of medicinal significance. Its rich reserves of vitamin C became a crucial supplement for combating widespread nutritional deficiencies, making it an essential component of wartime diets. This resurgence in its medicinal use reaffirmed its importance in human health and well-being, propelling it into the realm of modern medicine and nutritional research.

Contemporary Rediscovery and Sustainable Cultivation

In recent decades, the rosehip has experienced a revival, propelled by an increased interest in natural remedies, holistic wellness, and sustainable agriculture. Its historical significance, coupled with its diverse applications in modern cuisine and skincare, has rekindled a global fascination with this timeless botanical wonder. Furthermore, the emphasis on sustainable cultivation practices underscores the need to preserve its heritage and ecological importance for future generations.

The history of rosehips is a testament to the enduring relationship between humanity and nature, encapsulating a narrative of resilience, adaptation, and cultural significance. From ancient folklore to contemporary research, its journey reflects the timeless appeal and enduring relevance of this unassuming yet remarkable botanical treasure, underscoring its place as a symbol of human ingenuity and the enduring legacy of the natural world.

Understanding Rosehips

Rosehips, often referred to as the fruit of the rose plant, are the round, fleshy structures that develop below the petals of the flower. These small, vibrant fruits are part of the Rosa genus within the Rosaceae family and are renowned for their rich nutritional content and diverse applications in culinary, medicinal, and cosmetic fields.

A. Definition and Botanical Background:

Rosehips are the accessory fruit that forms after successful pollination of the rose flower. They typically appear in late summer to early autumn, varying in color from red to orange and even dark purple, depending on the specific species and maturity. Botanically, they develop from the receptacle of the rose flower, encompassing the seeds of the plant within their fleshy exterior. While often overlooked in favor of the ornamental beauty of the rose, rosehips hold a significant place in the botanical world due to their robust nutritional composition and historical significance in traditional medicine and culinary practices.

B. Types and Varieties of Rosehips:

The world of rosehips encompasses a diverse array of types and varieties, each distinguished by their unique characteristics and uses. Some of the commonly recognized varieties include the Rosa canina, known for its high vitamin C content and its extensive use in herbal medicine and skincare products. Additionally, the Rosa rugosa, characterized by its larger, deep red fruits, is renowned for its ornamental value and its use in the culinary arts. Other notable types, such as the Rosa moyesii and the Rosa rubiginosa, each bring their own distinct attributes, flavors, and applications, adding depth and diversity to the world of rosehips.

C. Natural Habitats and Cultivation:
Rosehips are naturally found in various regions across the globe, thriving in temperate climates and often found in the wild. They tend to flourish in areas with well-drained soil and ample sunlight, although some varieties exhibit a remarkable adaptability to different environments. These resilient fruits are commonly found in regions of Europe, Asia, and North America, often growing in hedgerows, woodland edges, and along roadsides. While they are known for their ability to thrive in the wild, rosehips are also cultivated in gardens and farms, with careful attention paid to soil quality, sunlight exposure, and proper pruning techniques to ensure optimal growth and fruit production. Cultivation practices often include the use of organic fertilizers and sustainable farming methods to preserve the integrity of the plant and its surrounding ecosystem.

Nutritional Value of Rosehips

A. Comprehensive Analysis of the Nutritional Composition:
Rosehips are renowned for their exceptional nutritional profile, encompassing a rich array of vitamins, minerals, and bioactive compounds that contribute to their health-promoting properties. They are notably high in vitamin C, containing significantly more of this essential nutrient than citrus fruits. Additionally, rosehips contain vitamins A, E, and K, as well as various B vitamins. They are also a valuable source of antioxidants such as flavonoids, carotenoids, and polyphenols, which play a crucial role in combating oxidative stress and reducing inflammation. Furthermore, they contain essential minerals such as iron, calcium, and magnesium, contributing to overall well-being and vitality.

B. Health Benefits and Medicinal Properties:
The nutritional richness of rosehips translates into a myriad of health benefits and medicinal properties. Their high vitamin C content supports immune function, aids in the absorption of iron, and promotes healthy skin, cartilage, and blood vessels. The presence of antioxidants helps protect the body from free radical damage, reducing the risk of chronic diseases such as heart disease and certain types of cancer. Rosehips are also known for their anti-inflammatory properties, making them valuable in alleviating symptoms associated with arthritis and joint pain. Additionally, their potential to lower cholesterol levels and regulate blood sugar makes them a promising natural remedy for managing cardiovascular health and diabetes.

C. Historical Uses in Traditional Medicine and Folklore:
Rosehips have a long history of use in traditional medicine, spanning various cultures and civilizations. Ancient societies recognized their medicinal properties and used them to treat a range of ailments, including colds, flu, digestive disorders, and skin conditions. They were often brewed into teas, syrups, or herbal extracts to harness their immune-boosting and anti-

4

inflammatory effects. Furthermore, the folklore surrounding rosehips often portrays them as symbols of protection, fertility, and vitality, with their inclusion in various rituals and ceremonies underscoring their cultural significance and enduring legacy in human history.

Understanding the nutritional value of rosehips not only underscores their role in promoting holistic well-being but also highlights their historical importance in traditional medicine and cultural folklore. These aspects collectively contribute to the continued exploration of their potential in contemporary health practices and the preservation of their rich botanical legacy.

Cultivation and Gardening of Rosehips

A. Guide to Growing Rosehips in Home Gardens and Commercial Farms:

1. Selection of Varieties: Choose suitable rosehip varieties based on climate and intended use, considering factors such as flavor, yield, and disease resistance.

2. Soil Preparation: Opt for well-drained, loamy soil with a slightly acidic pH for optimal growth. Incorporate organic matter and ensure adequate drainage to prevent waterlogging.

3. Planting: Plant rosehips in early spring or late fall, ensuring sufficient spacing between plants to allow for proper air circulation and sunlight exposure.

4. Sunlight and Watering: Place the plants in areas with ample sunlight, and water them regularly, especially during the growing season, while being cautious not to overwater.

5. Mulching and Fertilizing: Apply organic mulch to retain moisture and suppress weed growth. Use balanced fertilizers, preferably organic, to promote healthy growth and fruit production.

B. Best Practices for Nurturing and Maintaining Rosehip Plants:

1. Pruning: Regularly prune the plants to remove dead or diseased wood, promote new growth, and maintain an open structure for better air circulation.

2. Disease and Pest Management: Monitor the plants for common dis eases such as powdery mildew and rust, and employ appropriate organic treatments. Encourage natural predators to control pests, and use natural repellents to deter harmful insects.

3. Winter Protection: Shield the plants from harsh winter conditions by applying a layer of mulch around the base and, if necessary, using protective coverings or wraps to prevent frost damage.

4. Harvesting: Time the harvesting of rosehips when they reach their full color and are slightly soft to the touch. Use sharp shears to cut the fruits carefully, ensuring minimal damage to the plant.

C. Tips for Addressing Common Challenges and Pest Control:

1. Aphids and Mites: Introduce beneficial insects like ladybugs or use insecticidal soaps to control aphids and mites.

2. Powdery Mildew: Improve air circulation, avoid overhead watering, and apply fungicidal sprays with organic solutions like neem oil.

3. Rosehip Sawfly: Handpick the larvae, encourage natural predators, and apply horticultural oils or insecticidal soaps as a preventive measure.

4. Root Rot: Ensure proper drainage and avoid overwatering to prevent root rot, and use well-draining soil amendments if necessary.

By following these cultivation and gardening practices, both home gardeners and commercial farmers can foster healthy rosehip plants and ensure a bountiful harvest while effectively managing common challenges and promoting sustainable growth.

Harvesting and Processing Rosehips

A. Ideal Time for Harvesting:

1. Timing: Harvest rosehips in the late summer to early autumn, typically after the first frost, when the fruits have reached their full color and are slightly soft to the touch.

2. Color and Texture: Look for vibrant, deep-colored rosehips that appear plump and have a slight give when gently squeezed, indicating their readiness for picking.

3. Avoid Overripeness: Be cautious not to leave the fruits on the plant for too long, as overripeness can lead to a decrease in their nutritional value and flavor.

B. Techniques for Efficient and Sustainable Collection:

1. Handpicking: Handpick the rosehips carefully, using sharp shears to cut the fruits from the plant, ensuring minimal damage to the stems and surrounding foliage.

2. Sustainable Practices: Implement sustainable harvesting practices by only collecting a portion of the ripe fruits, allowing the remaining rosehips to mature fully and contribute to the ecosystem by providing food for wildlife.

C. Various Methods for Processing and Preservation:

1. Cleaning and Drying: Rinse the harvested rosehips thoroughly to remove any dirt or debris. Dry them either naturally in the sun or using a dehydrator until they are fully dehydrated and their moisture content is minimal.

2. Freezing: Freeze the cleaned and dried rosehips for long-term preservation, either whole or in pureed form, to retain their nutritional value and flavor.

3. Jam and Syrup Making: Use fresh or dried rosehips to make flavorful jams, jellies, or syrups, preserving their taste and nutritional benefits while creating versatile and long-lasting products.

4. Tea and Infusion Preparation: Dry the rosehips and use them to brew aromatic teas and infusions, capturing their rich flavors and health-promoting properties in a soothing and nourishing beverage.

By adhering to these recommended techniques for harvesting and processing rosehips, individuals can effectively preserve the fruits' nutritional value and extend their shelf life while minimizing waste and promoting sustainable practices in line with environmental conservation. Introduction to

Rosehips in Global Cuisine

Rosehips, often celebrated for their vibrant color and distinctively tart flavor, have garnered a place of prominence in the culinary traditions of various cultures worldwide. From the snow-capped peaks of the Himalayas to the sun-drenched Mediterranean coast, the versatile nature of rosehips has found its way into an array of culinary delights, enriching the gastronomic experiences of people across the globe.

A. Culinary Traditions Around the World: Exploring the Use of Rosehips in Different Cultures

Throughout history, diverse cultures have integrated rosehips into their traditional cuisines, harnessing their unique tanginess to elevate a myriad of dishes. From the fragrant rosehip-infused teas of the Middle East to the savory rosehip sauces of Scandinavian kitchens, the global tapestry of culinary traditions reflects the rich tapestry of flavors and techniques that have embraced the essence of rosehips in distinctive and delectable ways.

B. Fusion Cuisine: Blending Rosehips with Diverse Culinary Styles and Flavors

In the contemporary culinary landscape, chefs and home cooks alike are exploring the art of fusion cuisine, skillfully blending the tangy essence of rosehips with a diverse array of culinary styles and flavors. The marriage of rosehips with ingredients from across the globe has given rise to innovative dishes that harmoniously balance the fruit's tartness with the nuanced flavors of various culinary heritages, creating a delightful fusion that transcends cultural boundaries.

C. Gourmet Exploration: Showcasing Upscale and Innovative Rosehip-Based Dishes
In the realm of gourmet dining, the versatile nature of rosehips has inspired chefs to craft exquisite and innovative dishes, elevating the fruit to a position of luxury and sophistication. From delicate rosehip-infused sorbets to elegant entrees featuring rosehip reduction sauces, the world of haute cuisine has embraced the subtle complexities of rosehips, transforming them into culinary masterpieces that tantalize the palate and ignite the senses.

As we embark on a journey through the global culinary landscape, the exploration of rosehips in various cultural traditions, fusion cuisines, and gourmet creations invites us to savor the unique flavors and textures that this humble yet remarkable fruit has to offer. Through the lens of global cuisine, we discover the enduring appeal and the endless possibilities that rosehips bring to the art of gastronomy.

Rosehips have garnered rich symbolic significance in diverse societies across the globe, reflecting a tapestry of cultural beliefs, values, and traditions. In various cultures, these vibrant fruits carry profound meanings, representing themes of love, resilience, and transformation, and serving as potent symbols in the collective consciousness of humanity.

Symbolism and Cultural Significance in Different Societies

1. Love and Romance: In many societies, rosehips are emblematic of love and romance, often associated with the passion and intensity of romantic relationships. They symbolize deep affection, beauty, and the nurturing of emotional connections, embodying the tender and enduring aspects of love in different cultural contexts.

2. Resilience and Endurance: The hardiness of the rosehip plant and its ability to thrive in challenging environments have led to its symbolic association with resilience and endurance. In some cultures, the rosehip represents the ability to withstand adversity and emerge stronger, serving as a reminder of the strength inherent in overcoming obstacles and persevering through difficult times.

3. Vitality and Renewal: The rejuvenating properties of rosehips, enriched with essential nutrients and antioxidants, have positioned them as symbols of vitality and renewal in various societies. They are often linked to the concepts of rejuvenation, youthfulness, and the cyclic nature of life, emphasizing the importance of revitalization and the continuous process of growth and regeneration.

4. Beauty and Grace: The elegant and vibrant appearance of rosehips has led to their symbolic association with beauty and grace. They are often celebrated for their aesthetic appeal, serving as representations of natural beauty and elegance in different cultural narratives. Their inclusion in art, literature, and cultural practices highlights their enduring role as symbols of aesthetic appreciation and refinement.

5. Nurturing and Nourishment: Given their rich nutritional content and historical use as a source of sustenance, rosehips symbolize nourishment and nurturing in various cultures. They represent the provision of essential sustenance and care, underscoring the importance of nourishing the body, mind, and soul to foster growth, well-being, and holistic development.

Through their multifaceted symbolism, rosehips have become integral elements of cultural narratives, reflecting universal themes of love, resilience, vitality, beauty, and nourishment. Their significance in different societies underscores their profound impact on human perceptions and experiences, serving as timeless symbols that resonate with the complexities of the human condition.

Example of Rosehip Symbolism in Literature: Love and Romance

In literature, the symbolism of the rosehip has been employed to evoke themes of love, resilience, and the passage of time, often serving as a powerful metaphor for the complexities of human relationships. One notable example of the rosehip's symbolic significance can be found in the renowned poem "A Red, Red Rose" by Robert Burns, a celebrated Scottish poet from the 18th century.

In the final stanza of the poem, Burns writes:

"Till a' the seas gang dry, my dear,
And the rocks melt wi' the sun:
I will luve thee still, my dear,
While the sands o' life shall run."

Here, the enduring nature of the poet's love is likened to the timeless resilience of the rosehip, signifying a commitment that transcends the temporal constraints of life. The image of the "sands o' life" running, juxtaposed with the idea of the seas drying and the rocks melting, underscores the temporal fragility of human existence, while the promise of unwavering love remains steadfast and enduring, much like the resilience of the rosehip.

Through the use of the rosehip as a symbol, Burns conveys the idea of a love that perseveres through the trials and tribulations of life, reflecting the universal theme of enduring devotion and commitment that continues to resonate with readers across cultures and generations. The poem's use of the rosehip as a metaphor for enduring love serves to emphasize the timeless and transcendent nature of deep emotional connections that withstand the test of time.

Example of Rosehip Symbolism in Literature:
Resilience and Endurance

In literature, the symbolism of the rosehip as a representation of resilience and endurance is often portrayed through its ability to survive harsh conditions and bloom despite adversity. One notable example of this symbolism can be found in the novel "The Secret Garden" by Frances Hodgson Burnett, first published in 1911.

In the novel, the secret garden itself serves as a metaphor for rejuvenation and rebirth, while the hardy, resilient nature of the rosehip is used to symbolize the tenacity and perseverance of the characters, particularly that of the protagonist, Mary Lennox. As the story progresses, Mary, a lonely and neglected young girl, discovers the neglected secret garden, which she gradually nurtures back to life, much like she nurtures her own spirit.

The symbolism of the rosehip is exemplified in the character of the garden itself, as it begins to thrive under Mary's care, despite initially appearing barren and lifeless. The transformation of the garden, with the rosehip as one of its enduring symbols, parallels the emotional transformation and growth experienced by Mary as she learns to cultivate resilience and find joy in the face of adversity.

Through the depiction of the resilient and enduring nature of the rosehip within the context of the secret garden, Burnett communicates the profound message of the human spirit's capacity for renewal and transformation, emphasizing the power of perseverance, hope, and the ability to overcome life's challenges. This symbolism serves to inspire readers with the belief that, like the rosehip, they too can weather life's storms and blossom into their full potential, even in the harshest of conditions.

Example of Rosehip Symbolism in Literature:
Vitality and Renewal

In literature, the symbolism of the rosehip as a representation of vitality and renewal often serves as a metaphor for the resilience of the human spirit and the potential for personal growth and transformation. One poignant example of this symbolism can be found in the poem "The Waste Land" by T.S. Eliot, a seminal work of modernist poetry first published in 1922.

In the poem, Eliot utilizes the image of the rosehip to convey a sense of renewal and vitality amidst desolation and despair. In the section titled "What the Thunder Said," Eliot writes:

"Here is no water but only rock
Rock and no water and the sandy road
The road winding above among the mountains
Which are mountains of rock without water

If there were water we should stop and drink
Amongst the rock one cannot stop or think
Sweat is dry and feet are in the sand
If there were only water amongst the rock
Dead mountain mouth of carious teeth that cannot spit
Here one can neither stand nor lie nor sit
There is not even silence in the mountains
But dry sterile thunder without rain
There is not even solitude in the mountains
But red sullen faces sneer and snarl
From doors of mudcracked houses
If there were water
And no rock
If there were rock
And also water
And water
A spring
A pool among the rock
If there were the sound of water only
Not the cicada
And dry grass singing
But sound of water over a rock
Where the hermit-thrush sings in the pine trees
Drip drop drip drop drop drop drop
But there is no water"

The imagery of the barren and desolate landscape without water is contrasted with the image of water and the life-giving vitality it brings. The longing for water and the subsequent image of a spring or pool among the rocks symbolize the yearning for renewal and rejuvenation, highlighting the transformative power of nature's vitality amidst a barren and lifeless environment. This symbolism serves to underscore the enduring human desire for regeneration and the belief in the potential for new beginnings, even in the most desolate of circumstances.

Example of Rosehip Symbolism in Literature: Beauty and Grace

In literature, the symbolism of the rosehip as a representation of beauty and grace is often intertwined with themes of elegance, refinement, and the fleeting nature of life's pleasures. One striking example of this symbolism can be found in the poetic works of the English Romantic poet, John Keats. In his famous poem, "Ode to a Nightingale," published in 1819, Keats employs the image of the rosehip to convey a sense of beauty and transient joy.

In one of the stanzas, Keats writes:

"Thou wast not born for death, immortal Bird!
No hungry generations tread thee down;
The voice I hear this passing night was heard
In ancient days by emperor and clown:
Perhaps the self-same song that found a path
Through the sad heart of Ruth, when, sick for home,
She stood in tears amid the alien corn;
The same that oft-times hath
Charmed magic casements, opening on the foam
Of perilous seas, in faery lands forlorn."

Here, the poet's description of the enduring and timeless song of the nightingale is juxtaposed with the image of the rosehip, symbolizing the delicate and fleeting nature of beauty. The rosehip serves as a poignant reminder of life's transient pleasures, evoking a sense of longing and melancholy for the ephemeral moments of grace and elegance that are inevitably subject to the passage of time.

Example of Rosehip Symbolism in Literature: Nurturing and Nourishment

In literature, the symbolism of the rosehip as a representation of nurturing and nourishment often conveys themes of care, sustenance, and emotional nourishment. One poignant example of this symbolism can be found in the novel "The Secret Life of Bees" by Sue Monk Kidd, published in 2001.

In the novel, the nurturing and nourishing qualities of the rosehip are reflected in the character of August Boatwright, who tends to a thriving beehive and cultivates a sense of community and emotional healing within her surroundings. August's nurturing spirit, akin to the nourishing properties of the rosehip, serves as a source of comfort and sustenance for the protagonist, Lily Owens, a young girl struggling with the emotional burdens of her past.

Through the character of August, the novel emphasizes the transformative power of nurturing care and emotional nourishment, depicting the way in which a nurturing presence can provide solace and support, much like the nourishing properties of the rosehip. August's role as a nurturing figure highlights the significance of fostering emotional well-being and resilience, underscoring the profound impact of love, care, and support in fostering personal growth and healing.

The symbolism of the rosehip as a representation of nurturing and nourishment in "The Secret Life of Bees" serves to underscore the importance of emotional sustenance and the transformative power of nurturing relationships, ultimately conveying the message that through acts of kindness and care, individuals can find the strength and support needed to overcome life's adversities and thrive.

Folk Tales and Myths Associated with Rosehips

Folk tales and myths associated with rosehips often depict these vibrant fruits as symbols of enchantment, healing, and transformation. These stories, passed down through generations, highlight the mystical allure of rosehips and their significance in various cultural narratives. One such folk tale comes from Scandinavian folklore and involves the mystical powers of the rosehip.

In Scandinavian mythology, there is a tale of a group of forest spirits who guard a hidden grove of wild rosehip bushes. According to the legend, these rosehips possess the power to heal any ailment and grant eternal youth to those who consume them. However, the forest spirits are fiercely protective of the rosehips, and anyone attempting to pluck the fruits without their permission is said to be met with misfortune and eternal wandering within the enchanted forest.

The tale narrates the journey of a brave young adventurer who, determined to cure his ailing mother, embarks on a quest to find the elusive grove of rosehips. Along the way, he encounters various trials and tribulations, facing tests of courage, wisdom, and compassion. Eventually, through his perseverance and purity of heart, he gains the favor of the forest spirits, who guide him to the sacred grove.

In the grove, the young adventurer must demonstrate his reverence for nature and his understanding of the delicate balance between human desires and the needs of the natural world. Upon proving his worth, he is granted a handful of rosehips, which he uses to heal his mother and bring prosperity and vitality to his village. Through this tale, the rosehip is depicted as a symbol of not only physical healing but also spiritual enlightenment and the importance of respecting the natural world.

The folklore surrounding the mystical powers of rosehips serves to underscore their significance as agents of transformation and vitality in the cultural consciousness, highlighting their place as conduits of both physical and spiritual well-being in various folkloric traditions.

Two more examples of rosehips in world folklore:

1. **Persian Mythology:** In Persian folklore, there is a legend that tells the tale of a young maiden who was transformed into a rosehip bush by an envious sorceress. According to the myth, the maiden was known for her unparalleled beauty and kindness, which attracted the attention of the sorceress, who sought to diminish her radiance. As punishment for her perceived superiority, the sorceress cast a spell that turned the maiden into a rosehip bush, destined to bloom with vibrant and resilient fruits as a testament to her enduring spirit. The tale serves as a symbol of the transformative power of inner beauty and resilience in the face of adversity, emphasizing the notion that true radiance emanates from within.

2. **Native American Legends:** Among some Native American tribes, the rosehip is regarded as a sacred symbol of fertility and abundance. In certain creation

myths, the rosehip is believed to have emerged from the tears of a mother grieving for her lost children, signifying both the sorrow and the eventual renewal that arise from the cycle of life. The fruit's vibrant color and nourishing properties are often associated with the bountiful gifts of the earth, embodying the nurturing and life-giving aspects of nature. Additionally, the rosehip is sometimes featured in ceremonial practices, where it is used to invoke blessings and foster a connection with the natural world, highlighting its significance as a revered symbol of sustenance and spiritual harmony in Native American folklore.

Artistic Representation of Rosehips

Here are ten examples of specific artistic representations of rosehips, including mention of the works, artists, countries of origin, and years of creation:

1. Oil Paintings: "Bouquet of Rosehips" by Henri Fantin-Latour, created in France in 1875, is an exquisite example of a still life composition showcasing the vibrant colors and intricate details of rosehips.

2. Watercolor Illustrations: "Rosehips in Autumn" by Beatrix Potter, created in England in 1890, is a delicate watercolor depiction that captures the ethereal beauty of rosehips in their natural environment.

3. Botanical Drawings: "Rosa Canina" by Maria Sibylla Merian, created in the Netherlands in 1702, is a meticulously detailed botanical drawing that showcases the structural intricacies of rosehips for both scientific and artistic appreciation.

4. Ceramic Sculptures: "Rosehip Vase" by Clarice Cliff, created in the United Kingdom in 1930, is a stunning ceramic sculpture that embodies the organic contours and textures of rosehips, serving as a notable piece of Art Deco design.

5. Textile Art: "Rosehip Tapestry" by William Morris, created in England in 1883, is an intricately woven textile art piece that features the vibrant colors and organic shapes of rosehips within Morris's iconic textile designs.

6. Photography: "Rosehips in Winter" by Robert Mapplethorpe, created in the United States in 1986, is a fine art photograph that captures the stark beauty of frozen rosehips, showcasing their natural elegance and poetic symbolism.

7. Glass Blowing: "Rosehip Glass Sculpture" by Dale Chihuly, created in the United States in 1995, is an exquisite glass blowing masterpiece that skillfully captures the translucence and delicate forms of rosehips in a stunning three-dimensional glass sculpture.

8. Wood Carvings: "Rosehip Wooden Relief" by Grinling Gibbons, created in England in 1680, is an intricately carved wooden relief that highlights the natural curves and textures of rosehips, serving as a notable example of Baroque woodwork.

9. Metalwork: "Rosehip Metal Sculpture" by Albert Paley, created in the United States in 2010, is an intricate metalwork sculpture that emphasizes the elegance and intricate forms of rosehips through the skillful manipulation of metal materials.

10. Floral Arrangements: "Rosehip Bouquet" by Constance Spry, created in England in 1955, is an elaborate floral arrangement that incorporates fresh rosehips alongside other flowers, showcasing their vibrant colors and unique shapes in a visually stunning composition.

Culinary Applications of Rosehips

Throughout diverse cuisines and historic periods, the use of rosehips as a key ingredient has contributed to the development of unique flavors and culinary traditions, highlighting the enduring appeal and versatile nature of this vibrant fruit across different cultures and time periods. Some examples include:

1. Scandinavian Cuisine: Rosehips have been a key ingredient in Scandinavian cooking for centuries, with rosehip soups, jams, and sauces featuring prominently in traditional Nordic dishes.

2. Middle Eastern Cuisine: Rosehips have a long history of use in Middle Eastern cuisine, with their tangy flavor often incorporated into beverages, syrups, and desserts, dating back to ancient times.

3. Mediterranean Cuisine: Various cultures in the Mediterranean region have utilized rosehips in their culinary traditions, incorporating them into sauces, desserts, and herbal teas, dating back to ancient civilizations such as the Greeks and Romans.

4. Victorian Era Cuisine: During the Victorian era, rosehips were frequently used in jams, jellies, and syrups as a way to capture their unique flavor and benefit from their rich vitamin content, which was especially valued during a period with limited access to fresh fruits during certain seasons.

5. Renaissance Cuisine: Rosehips were also utilized in Renaissance cuisine, particularly in European royal courts, where they were incorporated into elaborate dishes, syrups, and medicinal concoctions, reflecting their valued status as a culinary and medicinal ingredient.

6. Ancient Chinese Cuisine: In ancient Chinese cuisine, rosehips were often used in various herbal teas, tonics, and medicinal preparations, reflecting their long-standing use in traditional Chinese medicine and culinary practices.

7. Indigenous American Cuisine: Some Indigenous American tribes historically used rosehips as a source of nutrition and medicinal benefits, incorporating them into teas, sauces, and dried preparations, highlighting their significance in indigenous culinary and medicinal traditions.

Health and Beauty Applications

Rosehips, renowned for their rich nutrient content and potent antioxidants, have been utilized for centuries in various health and beauty applications, offering a wide array of benefits for both internal wellness and external skincare. From nourishing the body with essential vitamins to rejuvenating the skin with their regenerative properties, rosehips have cemented their status as a versatile ingredient in the realms of health and beauty.

Health Benefits

1. Immune System Support: The high vitamin C content in rosehips promotes a robust immune system, helping to ward off infections and strengthen the body's natural defenses.

2. Anti-Inflammatory Properties: Rosehips contain polyphenols and anthocyanins, which possess anti-inflammatory properties that may help alleviate symptoms of inflammation-related conditions.

3. Digestive Health: The fiber content in rosehips aids in promoting healthy digestion and may contribute to improved gastrointestinal function and overall digestive well-being.

4. Joint Health: Studies suggest that the anti-inflammatory properties of rosehips may potentially help reduce joint pain and improve joint mobility, making them a valuable supplement for joint health.

Beauty Applications

1. Skincare: Rosehip oil, derived from the seeds of the fruit, is a popular natural skincare ingredient known for its hydrating and regenerative properties, helping to promote skin elasticity and reduce the appearance of scars and wrinkles.

2. Hair Care: The nourishing properties of rosehips are often harnessed in hair care products to promote scalp health, strengthen hair follicles, and improve the overall texture and appearance of the hair.

3. Aromatherapy: Rosehip essential oil, with its delicate floral scent, is used in aromatherapy to promote relaxation, reduce stress, and uplift the mood, contributing to overall emotional well-being and a sense of calm.

By harnessing the diverse health benefits and beauty applications of rosehips, individuals can integrate this versatile fruit into their wellness routines, both internally and externally, to promote holistic health, nourishment, and rejuvenation.

Culinary Rosehips

In the realm of culinary exploration, the vibrant and tangy essence of rosehips has long been celebrated for its ability to elevate a myriad of dishes, infusing them with a unique and tantalizing flavor profile.

From delectable jams and sauces to exquisite pastries and beverages, the culinary applications of rosehips offer a delightful journey through a world of exquisite tastes and aromatic delights. In this section, we embark on a culinary adventure that delves into the art of cooking and baking with rosehips, discovering the diverse and creative ways in which this humble fruit can transform ordinary recipes into extraordinary culinary masterpieces.

Through a fusion of traditional techniques and innovative culinary approaches, we explore the myriad possibilities that arise when the vibrant tanginess of rosehips harmonizes with a medley of flavors, creating a symphony of taste sensations that captivate the palate and ignite the senses.

Join us as we uncover the secrets of infusing your culinary creations with the essence of rosehips, unlocking a world of gastronomic wonders that promise to delight both the novice and the seasoned chef alike.

Rosehip Drinks Based on Ancient Cuisines

I. Georgian Rosehip Drink (Tkhilis Nivtsi)

Georgian Rosehip Drink, also known as Tkhilis Nivtsi, is a traditional beverage that holds a significant place in Georgian culinary culture. This invigorating drink is crafted from dried rosehips, which are renowned for their rich vitamin C content and tangy, slightly sweet flavor profile. Tkhilis Nivtsi embodies the essence of Georgian hospitality, often served as a welcoming refreshment to guests or enjoyed as a soothing elixir during colder months.

To prepare this ancient Georgian elixir, dried rosehips are gently simmered to extract their essence, resulting in a flavorful concoction that encapsulates the natural tanginess and subtle sweetness of the fruit. The addition of honey, cinnamon, and cloves infuses the drink with a delightful medley of aromatic and warming notes, creating a harmonious balance of flavors that evoke a sense of comfort and well-being.

Georgian Rosehip Drink is often enjoyed both warm and chilled, allowing its soothing properties to provide a sense of rejuvenation and vitality. Its vibrant hue, reminiscent of the Georgian countryside, serves as a visual testament to the abundance of nature's bounty and the rich culinary heritage of the region.

Whether sipped as a comforting tonic on a brisk evening or served as a welcoming gesture to friends and family, Georgian Rosehip Drink embodies the warmth of Georgian hospitality and the cherished tradition of enjoying simple yet wholesome pleasures.

Ingredients:
- 2 cups dried rosehips
- 6 cups water
- 1 cup honey
- 1 cinnamon stick
- 3-4 cloves
- 1-2 tablespoons freshly squeezed lemon juice
- Fresh mint leaves for garnish (optional)

Instructions:
1. Begin by rinsing the dried rosehips under cold water to remove any impurities.
2. In a large pot, combine the rosehips and water and bring to a boil over medium heat.
3. Once the water is boiling, reduce the heat and let the rosehips simmer for about 30-40 minutes, or until they become soft and tender.
4. Remove the pot from the heat and allow the rosehips to cool slightly.
5. Strain the mixture through a fine-mesh sieve or cheesecloth, pressing down on the rosehips to extract as much liquid as possible.
6. Return the strained liquid to the pot and add the honey, cinnamon stick, and cloves.
7. Bring the mixture to a gentle simmer and let it cook for an additional 15-20

minutes, allowing the flavors to meld together.

8. Remove the pot from the heat and stir in the freshly squeezed lemon juice.

9. Let the rosehip drink cool to room temperature before transferring it to a pitcher or individual serving glasses.

10. Refrigerate the drink for at least 2-3 hours before serving.

11. Serve the Georgian Rosehip Drink chilled, garnished with fresh mint leaves if desired, and enjoy the delightful blend of sweet, tangy, and aromatic flavors characteristic of this ancient Georgian beverage.

II. Rosehip Cup Spritz

The Rosehip Cup Spritz is a delightful and refreshing cocktail that marries the vibrant and fruity notes of the Rosehip Cup with the effervescence of sparkling wine and the crispness of soda water. This effervescent beverage offers a balanced fusion of floral, citrusy, and gently bitter flavors, creating a captivating sensory experience that is both invigorating and sophisticated.

To craft this enticing spritz, the Rosehip Cup, known for its delicate and fruity profile with hints of subtle bitterness, is combined with chilled sparkling wine, such as Prosecco or Champagne, to introduce a layer of effervescence and elegance. The addition of soda water lends a crisp and refreshing quality to the concoction, enhancing its lightness and drinkability.

Served over ice and garnished with fresh mint leaves or a twist of lemon, the Rosehip Cup Spritz presents a visually appealing and aromatic cocktail that is perfect for both casual gatherings and special occasions. Its delightful combination of flavors and textures makes it an ideal aperitif, stimulating the palate and setting the stage for a memorable dining experience.

Whether enjoyed during a leisurely afternoon gathering or as a prelude to an evening meal, the Rosehip Cup Spritz is a sophisticated and effervescent libation that embodies the art of mixology, celebrating the delicate nuances of the Rosehip Cup in a delightful and invigorating cocktail experience.

Ingredients:

- 50 ml Sacred Spirits' Rosehip Cup
- 100 ml sparkling wine (such as Prosecco or Champagne)
- 30 ml soda water
- Fresh mint leaves or a twist of lemon for garnish
- Ice cubes

Instructions:

1. Fill a large wine glass or a spritz glass with ice cubes to chill the glass.

2. Add the Sacred Spirits' Rosehip Cup to the glass, allowing it to chill alongside the ice.

3. Once the glass is adequately chilled, pour in the sparkling wine, followed by the soda water.

4. Give the mixture a gentle stir to ensure the ingredients are thoroughly combined.

5. Garnish the spritz with a sprig of fresh mint leaves or a twist of lemon, adding a

touch of aromatic freshness to the beverage.

6. Serve the Rosehip Cup Spritz immediately and enjoy its delightful blend of fruity, floral, and subtly bitter notes, making it an elegant and refreshing aperitif for any occasion.

III. Rosehip Tea

Rosehip tea has its roots in ancient civilizations, with historical accounts tracing its origins to ancient Persia and the Ottoman Empire. Revered for its medicinal properties and revered as a symbol of vitality and rejuvenation, this ancient brew was often prepared by steeping dried rosehips in hot water, harnessing their rich reservoir of nutrients and antioxidants.

Ancient healers and herbalists valued rosehip tea for its immune-boosting properties and its ability to promote overall well-being, considering it a precious elixir that could fortify the body and restore vitality. As time passed, the tradition of enjoying rosehip tea spread across various cultures, each embracing its unique therapeutic benefits and timeless allure. Even today, this ancient elixir continues to captivate tea enthusiasts and health-conscious individuals alike, carrying with it the legacy of centuries-old wisdom and the promise of wellness through the generations.

Rosehip tea, cherished for its robust flavor and wealth of health benefits, has a storied history dating back to ancient civilizations. This ancient elixir, revered for its high vitamin C content and its potential to boost the immune system, has been enjoyed for centuries as a soothing and nourishing beverage. To brew this ancient tonic, follow the recipe below:

Rosehip Tea Recipe:

Ingredients:
- 2 tablespoons dried rosehips
- 2 cups water
- Honey or sweetener of choice (optional)
- Lemon slices (optional)

Instructions:
1. In a saucepan, bring 2 cups of water to a gentle boil.
2. Add 2 tablespoons of dried rosehips to the boiling water.
3. Reduce the heat to low and let the rosehips simmer for 10-15 minutes, allowing the flavors to infuse into the water.
4. Remove the saucepan from the heat and strain the tea into a teapot or serving cup, discarding the used rosehips.
5. Add honey or your preferred sweetener to the tea if desired, stirring well to incorporate the sweetness.
6. Optionally, garnish the tea with a slice of lemon for an extra zing of citrusy flavor.

IV. Rosehip Mojito

While the Rosehip Mojito is a contemporary innovation, the concept of infusing beverages with the essence of rosehips can be traced back to ancient civilizations, including the ancient Egyptians and the Mayans. In these ancient cultures, rosehips were revered for their medicinal properties and were often incorporated into herbal tonics and elixirs believed to promote vitality and overall well-being. Over the centuries, the use of rosehips in beverages evolved, with cultures around the world embracing their tangy and fruity flavors, incorporating them into various culinary and mixology traditions. Today, the Rosehip Mojito stands as a testament to the enduring allure of this ancient fruit, captivating the senses with its vibrant flavors and paying homage to the time-honored legacy of rosehips in the realm of culinary innovation and libation craftsmanship.

The Rosehip Mojito is a contemporary twist on the classic Cuban cocktail, infusing the vibrant and tangy essence of rosehips into a refreshing and invigorating libation. This delightful concoction seamlessly blends the lively flavors of mint, lime, and rosehips, creating a harmonious fusion of citrusy and fruity notes that tantalize the taste buds. To prepare this modern interpretation of a beloved cocktail, follow the recipe below:

Rosehip Mojito Recipe:

Ingredients:
- 50ml white rum
- 25ml fresh lime juice
- 15ml rosehip syrup
- 6-8 fresh mint leaves
- Soda water
- Crushed ice
- Fresh rosehips and mint sprigs for garnish

Instructions:
1. In a cocktail shaker, gently muddle the mint leaves with the lime juice and rosehip syrup.
2. Add the white rum and a handful of crushed ice to the shaker.
3. Vigorously shake the mixture to combine the ingredients and chill the concoction.
4. Strain the mixture into a highball glass filled with fresh ice.
5. Top off the glass with soda water to add a sparkling effervescence.
6. Garnish the cocktail with fresh rosehips and a sprig of mint for a visually appealing presentation.

V. Rosehip Gin and Tonic

The use of rosehips in tonic beverages traces back to ancient civilizations such as the Ancient Egyptians and the Mayans, who revered the fruit for its potential health benefits and its rich reservoir of vitamins and antioxidants. Throughout history, rosehips have been integrated into various elixirs and tonics, valued for their rejuvenating and immune-boosting properties. Today, the Rosehip Gin and Tonic serves as a contemporary testament to this ancient tradition, capturing the essence of the past while infusing a modern cocktail with the timeless allure of the rosehip. By combining the vibrant flavors of the fruit with the botanical depth of gin and the effervescence of tonic water, this cocktail embodies a harmonious blend of ancient wisdom and contemporary mixology, inviting enthusiasts to savor a truly distinctive and invigorating libation.

The Rosehip Gin and Tonic is a modern twist on the classic cocktail, infusing the zesty and floral flavors of rosehips into the beloved concoction. This contemporary libation pays homage to the ancient use of rosehips in traditional herbal tonics and elixirs, showcasing the enduring appeal of this ancient fruit in the realm of mixology. Follow the recipe below to craft this refreshing and aromatic cocktail:

Rosehip Gin and Tonic Recipe:

Ingredients:
- 50ml gin
- 25ml rosehip syrup
- Tonic water
- Fresh rosehips and a wedge of lime for garnish
- Ice cubes

Instructions:
1. Fill a highball glass with ice cubes to chill the glass.
2. Add the gin and rosehip syrup to the glass.
3. Stir gently to combine the ingredients.
4. Top off the glass with tonic water, adding a refreshing effervescence to the cocktail.
5. Garnish with fresh rosehips and a wedge of lime for an extra burst of citrusy flavor.

VI. Rosehip and Hibiscus Tea

The consumption of herbal infusions, including rosehip and hibiscus-based teas, dates back to ancient civilizations such as Ancient Egypt, Ancient China, and the Mayan civilization. These ancient cultures valued the natural properties of herbs and flowers, often using them for their potential health benefits and their soothing properties. Rosehip and hibiscus were believed to possess rejuvenating and revitalizing qualities, with some cultures embracing them for their potential to promote overall well-being and vitality. Today, the tradition of brewing Rosehip and Hibiscus Tea continues, honoring the ancient wisdom that recognized the inherent value of these botanical ingredients and their contribution to a balanced and wholesome lifestyle.

Rosehip and Hibiscus Tea is a delightful herbal infusion that harmoniously blends the vibrant tartness of hibiscus with the sweet and tangy essence of rosehips, resulting in a visually striking and flavorful brew that has been enjoyed for centuries. This tea not only captivates the senses with its deep crimson hue and alluring aroma but also offers a range of potential health benefits, making it a cherished elixir among tea enthusiasts.

To prepare this delightful infusion, follow the recipe below:

Ingredients:

- 1 tablespoon dried rosehips
- 1 tablespoon dried hibiscus flowers
- 2 cups water
- Honey or sweetener of choice, to taste (optional)
- Fresh lemon slices or mint leaves for garnish (optional)

Instructions:

1. In a saucepan, bring 2 cups of water to a boil.
2. Add the dried rosehips and hibiscus flowers to the boiling water.
3. Reduce the heat to low and let the ingredients simmer for 5-10 minutes, allowing the flavors to infuse into the water.
4. Once the tea has reached your desired strength, remove the saucepan from the heat.
5. Strain the tea into a teapot or serving cup to remove the used herbs.
6. Sweeten the tea with honey or your preferred sweetener if desired, stirring well to incorporate the sweetness.
7. Optionally, garnish the tea with fresh lemon slices or mint leaves to enhance the flavor and add a decorative touch.

VII. Rosehip and Mint Tea

The tradition of infusing teas with herbs and botanicals has a rich history that spans ancient civilizations, including Ancient Egypt, Greece, and China, where the use of natural ingredients in teas was valued for its potential to promote well-being and balance. Both rosehips and mint were revered for their revitalizing and soothing properties, with mint often celebrated for its digestive benefits and rosehips cherished for their high vitamin content and potential immune-boosting qualities. Today, the practice of brewing Rosehip and Mint Tea honors this ancient legacy, showcasing the enduring appeal of these natural ingredients and their timeless contribution to the art of tea-making and holistic wellness.

Rosehip and Mint Tea is a soothing and aromatic herbal infusion that combines the bright and tangy flavor of rosehips with the refreshing coolness of mint. This timeless concoction, cherished for its invigorating taste and potential health benefits, has roots that trace back to ancient civilizations, where the use of herbs and botanicals in teas was valued for its therapeutic properties and aromatic allure. To prepare this ancient elixir, follow the recipe below:

Ingredients:

- 1 tablespoon dried rosehips
- 1 tablespoon fresh or dried mint leaves
- 2 cups water
- Honey or sweetener of choice, to taste (optional)
- Fresh lemon slices for garnish (optional)

Instructions:

1. In a saucepan, bring 2 cups of water to a boil.
2. Add the dried rosehips and mint leaves to the boiling water.
3. Reduce the heat to low and let the ingredients simmer for 5-10 minutes to allow the flavors to infuse into the water.
4. Once the tea has reached your desired strength, remove the saucepan from the heat.
5. Strain the tea into a teapot or serving cup to remove the used herbs.
6. Sweeten the tea with honey or your preferred sweetener if desired, stirring well to incorporate the sweetness.
7. Optionally, garnish the tea with fresh lemon slices to add a citrusy twist and enhance the overall flavor profile.

VIII. Rosehip and Ginger Tea

The practice of infusing teas with herbs and spices has ancient origins, with historical accounts tracing back to ancient civilizations such as Ancient China, India, and Egypt. Both rosehips and ginger were highly regarded for their potential medicinal properties, with ginger revered for its digestive and warming qualities, and rosehips valued for their high vitamin C content and their potential immune-boosting benefits. Today, the tradition of brewing Rosehip and Ginger Tea pays homage to this ancient legacy, celebrating the enduring allure of these natural ingredients and their timeless contribution to the art of tea-making and holistic wellness.

Rosehip and Ginger Tea is a warming and invigorating herbal infusion that combines the tangy sweetness of rosehips with the spicy and aromatic notes of ginger. This timeless elixir has a rich history that dates back to ancient civilizations, where the use of herbs and spices in teas was valued for its potential health benefits and its comforting and soothing properties. To brew this ancient tonic, follow the recipe below:

Ingredients:

- 1 tablespoon dried rosehips
- 1 teaspoon freshly grated ginger root
- 2 cups water
- Honey or sweetener of choice, to taste (optional)
- Fresh lemon slices for garnish (optional)

Instructions:

1. In a saucepan, bring 2 cups of water to a boil.
2. Add the dried rosehips and freshly grated ginger to the boiling water.
3. Reduce the heat to low and let the ingredients simmer for 10-15 minutes, allowing the flavors to infuse into the water.
4. Once the tea has reached your desired strength, remove the saucepan from the heat.
5. Strain the tea into a teapot or serving cup to remove the used herbs.

6. Sweeten the tea with honey or your preferred sweetener if desired, stirring well to incorporate the sweetness.
7. Optionally, garnish the tea with fresh lemon slices to add a citrusy twist and enhance the overall flavor profile.

IX. Rosehip and Cinnamon Tea

The practice of infusing teas with herbs and spices has ancient origins, with historical accounts dating back to ancient civilizations such as Ancient Egypt, Greece, and China. Both rosehips and cinnamon were highly esteemed for their potential medicinal properties, with cinnamon prized for its warming and digestive qualities, and rosehips valued for their high vitamin C content and their potential immune-boosting benefits. Today, the tradition of brewing Rosehip and Cinnamon Tea pays homage to this ancient legacy, celebrating the enduring allure of these natural ingredients and their timeless contribution to the art of tea-making and holistic wellness.

Rosehip and Cinnamon Tea is a comforting and aromatic herbal infusion that seamlessly blends the tangy sweetness of rosehips with the warm and spicy essence of cinnamon. This ancient elixir has a rich history that can be traced back to ancient civilizations, where the use of herbs and spices in teas was cherished for its potential health benefits and its ability to provide warmth and comfort. To prepare this ancient tonic, follow the recipe below:

Ingredients:

- 1 tablespoon dried rosehips
- 1 cinnamon stick or 1 teaspoon ground cinnamon
- 2 cups water
- Honey or sweetener of choice, to taste (optional)
- Fresh lemon slices for garnish (optional)

Instructions:

1. In a saucepan, bring 2 cups of water to a boil.
2. Add the dried rosehips and the cinnamon stick or ground cinnamon to the boiling water.
3. Reduce the heat to low and let the ingredients simmer for 10-15 minutes, allowing the flavors to infuse into the water.
4. Once the tea has reached your desired strength, remove the saucepan from the heat.
5. Strain the tea into a teapot or serving cup to remove the used herbs.
6. Sweeten the tea with honey or your preferred sweetener if desired, stirring well to incorporate the sweetness.
7. Optionally, garnish the tea with fresh lemon slices to add a citrusy twist and enhance the overall flavor profile.

X. Rosehip and Vanilla Tea

The tradition of infusing teas with herbs and spices has ancient origins, with historical accounts dating back to ancient civilizations such as Ancient Egypt, Greece, and China. Both rosehips and vanilla were highly esteemed for their potential medicinal properties, with vanilla prized for its aromatic and soothing qualities, and rosehips valued for their high vitamin C content and their potential immune-boosting benefits. Today, the tradition of brewing Rosehip and Vanilla Tea pays homage to this ancient legacy, celebrating the enduring allure of these natural ingredients and their timeless contribution to the art of tea-making and holistic wellness.

Rosehip and Vanilla Tea is a delightful and aromatic herbal infusion that combines the vibrant and tangy notes of rosehips with the rich and comforting essence of vanilla. This ancient elixir has roots that trace back to ancient civilizations, where the use of herbs and spices in teas was cherished for its potential health benefits and its ability to provide comfort and relaxation. To brew this ancient tonic, follow the recipe below:

Ingredients:

- 1 tablespoon dried rosehips
- 1 vanilla bean or 1 teaspoon pure vanilla extract
- 2 cups water
- Honey or sweetener of choice, to taste (optional)
- Fresh lemon slices for garnish (optional)

Instructions:

1. In a saucepan, bring 2 cups of water to a boil.
2. Add the dried rosehips and the split vanilla bean or pure vanilla extract to the boiling water.
3. Reduce the heat to low and let the ingredients simmer for 10-15 minutes, allowing the flavors to infuse into the water.
4. Once the tea has reached your desired strength, remove the saucepan from the heat.
5. Strain the tea into a teapot or serving cup to remove the used herbs.
6. Sweeten the tea with honey or your preferred sweetener if desired, stirring well to incorporate the sweetness.
7. Optionally, garnish the tea with fresh lemon slices to add a citrusy twist and enhance the overall flavor profile.

XI. Rosehip and Lemonade

The tradition of creating fruit-based beverages with herbs and spices has ancient origins, with historical accounts dating back to ancient civilizations such as Ancient Egypt, Greece, and Rome. Both rosehips and lemon were highly esteemed for their potential medicinal properties, with lemon prized for its refreshing and detoxifying qualities, and rosehips valued for their high vitamin C content and their potential immune-boosting benefits. Today, the tradition of crafting Rosehip and Lemonade pays homage to this ancient legacy, celebrating the enduring allure of these natural ingredients and their timeless contribution to the art of beverage-making and holistic wellness.

Rosehip and Lemonade is a delightful and refreshing beverage that combines the tangy sweetness of rosehips with the vibrant and citrusy zest of lemon. This ancient elixir has a rich history that can be traced back to ancient civilizations, where the use of fruits and herbs in beverages was cherished for its potential health benefits and its ability to provide a revitalizing and invigorating experience. To prepare this ancient tonic, follow the recipe below:

Ingredients:

- 1 cup fresh or dried rosehips
- 1 cup freshly squeezed lemon juice
- 4 cups water
- Honey or sweetener of choice, to taste (optional)
- Fresh mint leaves or lemon slices for garnish (optional)
- Ice cubes

Instructions:

1. In a saucepan, bring 4 cups of water to a boil.
2. Add the fresh or dried rosehips to the boiling water and let it simmer for 20-25 minutes.
3. Strain the rosehip infusion into a pitcher, discarding the used rosehips.
4. Add the freshly squeezed lemon juice to the rosehip infusion, stirring well to combine the flavors.
5. Sweeten the lemonade with honey or your preferred sweetener if desired, stirring until the sweetener is fully dissolved.
6. Chill the rosehip and lemonade mixture in the refrigerator for at least 1-2 hours.
7. Serve the Rosehip and Lemonade over ice, garnishing with fresh mint leaves or lemon slices for an extra burst of freshness and visual appeal.

XII. Rosehip and Orange Juice

The tradition of creating fruit-based beverages with herbs and spices has ancient origins, with historical accounts dating back to ancient civilizations such as Ancient Egypt, Greece, and Rome. Both rosehips and oranges were highly esteemed for their potential medicinal properties, with oranges prized for their immune-boosting and energizing qualities, and rosehips valued for their high vitamin C content and their potential benefits for overall well-being. Today, the tradition of crafting Rosehip and Orange Juice pays homage to this ancient legacy, celebrating the enduring allure of these natural ingredients and their timeless contribution to the art of beverage-making and holistic wellness.

Rosehip and Orange Juice is a vibrant and vitamin-rich beverage that combines the tangy sweetness of rosehips with the bright and citrusy flavors of oranges. This ancient elixir has roots that can be traced back to ancient civilizations, where the use of fruits and herbs in beverages was valued for its potential health benefits and its refreshing and rejuvenating properties. To prepare this ancient tonic, follow the recipe below:

Ingredients:

- 1 cup fresh or dried rosehips
- 1 cup freshly squeezed orange juice
- 4 cups water
- Honey or sweetener of choice, to taste (optional)
- Fresh mint leaves or orange slices for garnish (optional)
- Ice cubes

Instructions:

1. In a saucepan, bring 4 cups of water to a boil.
2. Add the fresh or dried rosehips to the boiling water and let it simmer for 20-25 minutes.
3. Strain the rosehip infusion into a pitcher, discarding the used rosehips.
4. Add the freshly squeezed orange juice to the rosehip infusion, stirring well to combine the flavors.
5. Sweeten the juice with honey or your preferred sweetener if desired, stirring until the sweetener is fully dissolved.
6. Chill the rosehip and orange juice mixture in the refrigerator for at least 1-2 hours.
7. Serve the Rosehip and Orange Juice over ice, garnishing with fresh mint leaves or orange slices for an extra burst of freshness and visual appeal.

XIII. Rosehip and Apple Cider

The practice of creating fruit-based beverages with herbs and spices has ancient origins, with historical accounts dating back to ancient civilizations such as Ancient Egypt, Greece, and Rome. Both rosehips and apples were highly esteemed for their potential health benefits, with apples valued for their refreshing and hydrating qualities, and rosehips revered for their high vitamin C content and their potential immune-boosting properties. Today, the tradition of crafting Rosehip and Apple Cider pays homage to this ancient legacy, celebrating the enduring allure of these natural ingredients and their timeless contribution to the art of beverage-making and holistic wellness.
XIII. Rosehip and Apple Cider

Rosehip and Apple Cider is a delightful and invigorating beverage that combines the tangy sweetness of rosehips with the crisp and refreshing taste of apple cider. This ancient elixir has a rich history that can be traced back to ancient civilizations, where the use of fruits and herbs in beverages was cherished for its potential health benefits and its ability to provide comfort and nourishment. To prepare this ancient tonic, follow the recipe below:

Ingredients:

- 1 cup fresh or dried rosehips
- 2 cups apple cider

- 2 cups water
- Honey or sweetener of choice, to taste (optional)
- Fresh apple slices or cinnamon sticks for garnish (optional)
- Ice cubes

Instructions:

1. In a saucepan, bring 2 cups of water to a boil.
2. Add the fresh or dried rosehips to the boiling water and let it simmer for 20-25 minutes.
3. Strain the rosehip infusion into a pitcher, discarding the used rosehips.
4. Add the apple cider to the rosehip infusion, stirring well to combine the flavors.
5. Sweeten the mixture with honey or your preferred sweetener if desired, stirring until the sweetener is fully dissolved.
6. Chill the rosehip and apple cider blend in the refrigerator for at least 1-2 hours.
7. Serve the Rosehip and Apple Cider over ice, garnishing with fresh apple slices or cinnamon sticks for an extra burst of flavor and visual appeal.

XIV. Rosehip and Pomegranate Juice

The tradition of creating fruit-based beverages with herbs and spices has ancient origins, with historical accounts dating back to various ancient civilizations such as Ancient Egypt, Greece, and Persia. Both rosehips and pomegranates were highly esteemed for their potential health benefits, with pomegranates valued for their antioxidant properties and rosehips revered for their high vitamin C content and their potential immune-boosting benefits. Today, the tradition of crafting Rosehip and Pomegranate Juice pays homage to this ancient legacy, celebrating the enduring allure of these natural ingredients and their timeless contribution to the art of beverage-making and holistic wellness

Rosehip and Pomegranate Juice is a vibrant and antioxidant-rich beverage that combines the tangy sweetness of rosehips with the bold and fruity flavors of pomegranate. This ancient elixir has roots that can be traced back to various ancient civilizations, where the use of fruits and herbs in beverages was valued for their potential health benefits and their refreshing and rejuvenating properties. To prepare this ancient tonic, follow the recipe below:

Ingredients:

- 1 cup fresh or dried rosehips
- 1 cup pomegranate juice
- 4 cups water
- Honey or sweetener of choice, to taste (optional)
- Fresh mint leaves or pomegranate arils for garnish (optional)
- Ice cubes

Instructions:

1. In a saucepan, bring 4 cups of water to a boil.
2. Add the fresh or dried rosehips to the boiling water and let it simmer for 20-25 minutes.
3. Strain the rosehip infusion into a pitcher, discarding the used rosehips.
4. Add the pomegranate juice to the rosehip infusion, stirring well to combine the flavors.
5. Sweeten the juice with honey or your preferred sweetener if desired, stirring until the sweetener is fully dissolved.
6. Chill the rosehip and pomegranate juice blend in the refrigerator for at least 1-2 hours.
7. Serve the Rosehip and Pomegranate Juice over ice, garnishing with fresh mint leaves or pomegranate arils for an extra burst of freshness and visual appeal.

XV. Rosehip and Honey Tea Recipe

The art of infusing teas with herbs and natural sweeteners dates back to numerous ancient civilizations, such as those in Ancient Egypt, Greece, and China. Honey, revered for its healing and antibacterial properties, was cherished alongside rosehips, esteemed for their high vitamin C content and immune-boosting capabilities. Today, brewing Rosehip and Honey Tea commemorates this ancient tradition, honoring the enduring allure of these natural ingredients and their timeless contribution to the art of tea-making and holistic well-being.

Rosehip and Honey Tea, a comforting and nourishing herbal infusion, marries the tangy sweetness of rosehips with the luscious, soothing touch of honey. This time-honored elixir traces back to various ancient civilizations, where the use of herbs and natural sweeteners in teas was treasured for their potential health benefits and their ability to provide solace and warmth. To savor this ancient tonic, follow the recipe below:

Ingredients:

- 1 tablespoon dried rosehips
- 1 teaspoon honey
- 1 cup water
- Fresh lemon slices for garnish (optional)

Instructions:

1. Bring 1 cup of water to a boil in a saucepan.
2. Add the dried rosehips, allowing them to simmer in the water for 5-10 minutes.
3. Strain the rosehip infusion into a teacup or mug, removing the used rosehips.
4. Stir in a teaspoon of honey, blending it well to heighten the sweetness.
5. For a twist, add a dash of cinnamon or a sprig of fresh mint to elevate the flavors.
6. Optionally, garnish the tea with fresh lemon slices to infuse a citrusy zest and enhance the overall aroma.

XVI. Rosehip and Chamomile Tea

The tradition of infusing teas with herbs and botanicals has ancient origins, with historical accounts dating back to various ancient civilizations such as Ancient Egypt, Greece, and Rome. Both rosehips and chamomile were highly esteemed for their potential medicinal properties, with chamomile cherished for its calming and soothing qualities, and rosehips valued for their high vitamin C content and their potential immune-boosting benefits. Today, the tradition of crafting Rosehip and Chamomile Tea pays homage to this ancient legacy, celebrating the enduring allure of these natural ingredients and their timeless contribution to the art of tea-making and holistic wellness.

Rosehip and Chamomile Tea is a soothing and aromatic herbal infusion that combines the tangy sweetness of rosehips with the calming and floral notes of chamomile. This timeless elixir has roots that can be traced back to ancient civilizations, where the use of herbs and botanicals in teas was cherished for their potential health benefits and their ability to provide relaxation and comfort. To prepare this ancient tonic, follow the recipe below:

Ingredients:

- 1 tablespoon dried rosehips
- 1 tablespoon dried chamomile flowers
- 2 cups water
- Honey or sweetener of choice, to taste (optional)
- Fresh lemon slices or chamomile flowers for garnish (optional)

Instructions:

1. In a saucepan, bring 2 cups of water to a boil.
2. Add the dried rosehips and chamomile flowers to the boiling water.
3. Reduce the heat to low and let the ingredients simmer for 5-10 minutes, allowing the flavors to infuse into the water.
4. Once the tea has reached your desired strength, remove the saucepan from the heat.
5. Strain the tea into a teapot or serving cup to remove the used herbs.
6. Sweeten the tea with honey or your preferred sweetener if desired, stirring well to incorporate the sweetness.
7. Optionally, garnish the tea with fresh lemon slices or chamomile flowers for an extra burst of flavor and visual appeal.

XVII. Rosehip and Lavender Tea

The tradition of blending teas with herbs and flowers has ancient origins, with historical accounts dating back to civilizations such as Ancient Egypt, Greece, and China. Lavender, cherished for its aromatic and calming properties, was highly esteemed alongside rosehips, valued for their high vitamin C content and potential immune-boosting benefits. Today, the practice of preparing Rosehip and Lavender Tea honors this ancient legacy, celebrating the enduring allure of these natural ingredients and their timeless contribution to the art of tea-making and holistic wellness. Rosehip and Lavender Tea is a fragrant and soothing herbal blend that combines the tangy sweetness of rosehips with the delicate floral notes of lavender. This revered elixir has ancient roots that can be traced back to various civilizations, where the use of herbs and flowers in teas was treasured for their potential health benefits and their ability to promote relaxation and tranquility. To prepare this timeless tonic, follow the recipe below:

Ingredients:

- 1 tablespoon dried rosehips
- 1 teaspoon dried lavender buds
- 2 cups water
- Honey or sweetener of choice, to taste (optional)
- Fresh lemon slices or lavender sprigs for garnish (optional)

Instructions:

1. In a saucepan, bring 2 cups of water to a boil.
2. Add the dried rosehips and lavender buds to the boiling water.
3. Reduce the heat to low and let the ingredients simmer for 5-10 minutes, allowing the flavors to meld with the water.
4. Once the tea has reached your desired strength, remove the saucepan from the heat.
5. Strain the tea into a teapot or serving cup to remove the used herbs.
6. Sweeten the tea with honey or your preferred sweetener if desired, stirring well to incorporate the sweetness.
7. Optionally, garnish the tea with fresh lemon slices or sprigs of lavender for an added touch of freshness and visual appeal.

Benefits of Lavender:

Lavender is known for its potential health benefits, including its ability to promote relaxation and reduce stress and anxiety. It is also believed to aid in digestion and support healthy sleep patterns. Additionally, lavender possesses anti-inflammatory and antimicrobial properties, contributing to its role in traditional and holistic medicine for centuries. When combined with the nutritious qualities of rosehips, lavender can enhance the overall wellness benefits of this delightful herbal infusion.

XVIII. Rosehip and Sage Tea

Sage, revered for its distinctive flavor and potential health benefits, was highly regarded alongside rosehips, valued for their high vitamin C content and immune-boosting properties. Today, brewing Rosehip and Sage Tea pays homage to this ancient legacy, celebrating the enduring allure of these natural ingredients and their timeless contribution to the art of tea-making and holistic wellness.

Rosehip and Sage Tea is a flavorful and aromatic herbal fusion that combines the tangy sweetness of rosehips with the earthy and herbaceous notes of sage. This cherished elixir has ancient origins, harking back to various civilizations, where the use of herbs and botanicals in teas was esteemed for their potential health benefits and their unique flavor profiles. To prepare this timeless tonic, follow the recipe below:

Ingredients:

- 1 tablespoon dried rosehips
- 1 teaspoon dried sage leaves
- 2 cups water
- Honey or sweetener of choice, to taste (optional)
- Fresh lemon slices or sage leaves for garnish (optional)

Instructions:

1. In a saucepan, bring 2 cups of water to a boil.
2. Add the dried rosehips and sage leaves to the boiling water.
3. Reduce the heat to low and let the ingredients simmer for 5-10 minutes, allowing the flavors to infuse into the water.
4. Once the tea has reached your desired strength, remove the saucepan from the heat.
5. Strain the tea into a teapot or serving cup to remove the used herbs.
6. Sweeten the tea with honey or your preferred sweetener if desired, stirring well to incorporate the sweetness.
7. Optionally, garnish the tea with fresh lemon slices or sage leaves for an added hint of zest and visual appeal.

XIX. Rosehip and Thyme Tea

Thyme, cherished for its distinctive flavor and potential health benefits, was highly regarded alongside rosehips, valued for their high vitamin C content and immune-boosting properties. Today, the practice of preparing Rosehip and Thyme Tea pays homage to this ancient legacy, celebrating the enduring allure of these natural ingredients and their timeless contribution to the art of tea-making and holistic wellness.

Rosehip and Thyme Tea is a delightful and aromatic herbal blend that combines the tangy sweetness of rosehips with the earthy and slightly minty notes of thyme. This revered elixir has ancient origins, with roots that can be traced back to various civilizations, where the use of herbs and botanicals in teas was treasured for their potential health benefits and their refreshing and invigorating properties. To prepare this timeless tonic, follow the recipe below:

Ingredients:

- 1 tablespoon dried rosehips
- 1 teaspoon dried thyme leaves
- 2 cups water
- Honey or sweetener of choice, to taste (optional)
- Fresh lemon slices or thyme sprigs for garnish (optional)

Instructions:

1. In a saucepan, bring 2 cups of water to a boil.
2. Add the dried rosehips and thyme leaves to the boiling water.
3. Reduce the heat to low and let the ingredients simmer for 5-10 minutes, allowing the flavors to infuse into the water.
4. Once the tea has reached your desired strength, remove the saucepan from the heat.
5. Strain the tea into a teapot or serving cup to remove the used herbs.
6. Sweeten the tea with honey or your preferred sweetener if desired, stirring well to incorporate the sweetness.
7. Optionally, garnish the tea with fresh lemon slices or thyme sprigs for an added touch of freshness and visual appeal.

XX. Rosehip and Elderflower Tea

Elderflower, cherished for its delicate flavor and potential health benefits, was highly regarded alongside rosehips, valued for their high vitamin C content and immune-boosting properties. Today, brewing Rosehip and Elderflower Tea pays homage to this ancient legacy, celebrating the enduring allure of these natural ingredients and their timeless contribution to the art of tea-making and holistic wellness.

Rosehip and Elderflower Tea is a delicate and fragrant herbal blend that harmoniously combines the tangy sweetness of rosehips with the floral and aromatic notes of elderflower. This revered elixir has ancient origins, dating back to various civilizations, where the use of herbs and flowers in teas was treasured for their potential health benefits and their refreshing and calming properties. To prepare this timeless tonic, follow the recipe below:

Ingredients:

- 1 tablespoon dried rosehips
- 1 teaspoon dried elderflowers
- 2 cups water
- Honey or sweetener of choice, to taste (optional)
- Fresh lemon slices or elderflowers for garnish (optional)

Instructions:

1. In a saucepan, bring 2 cups of water to a boil.
2. Add the dried rosehips and elderflowers to the boiling water.
3. Reduce the heat to low and let the ingredients simmer for 5-10 minutes, allowing the flavors to infuse into the water.
4. Once the tea has reached your desired strength, remove the saucepan from the heat.
5. Strain the tea into a teapot or serving cup to remove the used herbs.
6. Sweeten the tea with honey or your preferred sweetener if desired, stirring well to incorporate the sweetness.
7. Optionally, garnish the tea with fresh lemon slices or elderflowers for an added touch of vibrancy and visual appeal.

Ancient Greek Method of Making Rosehip Wine

This ancient Greek method of making rosehip wine involves boiling the rosehips to extract their flavor and nutrients, then fermenting the mixture with sugar and wine yeast to create a sweet and fruity wine. The wine is then aged for at least 6 months to allow the flavors to develop.

Ingredients:

- 2 pounds fresh rosehips
- 2 pounds sugar
- 1 gallon water
- 1 package wine yeast

Instructions:

1. Wash the rosehips and remove the stems and blossom ends.
2. Crush the rosehips with a potato masher or rolling pin to break the flesh a little.
3. Place the crushed rosehips in a large pot and add 1 gallon of water.
4. Bring the mixture to a boil, then reduce the heat and simmer for 30 minutes.
5. Remove the pot from the heat and let it cool to room temperature.
6. Strain the mixture through a cheesecloth or fine mesh strainer, pressing on the solids to extract as much liquid as possible.
7. Return the liquid to the pot and add 2 pounds of sugar.
8. Heat the mixture over low heat, stirring until the sugar dissolves.
9. Remove the pot from the heat and let it cool to room temperature.
10. Add the wine yeast to the mixture and stir well.
11. Pour the mixture into a sterilized fermenting bucket and cover with a lid or cloth.
12. Let the mixture ferment for 7-10 days, stirring daily.
13. Strain the mixture through a cheesecloth or fine mesh strainer and transfer the liquid to a sterilized carboy.
14. Let the wine age for at least 6 months before bottling.

Fifty Rosehip Cocktails with International Influences

In the realm of mixology, the alluring essence of rosehip has transcended cultural boundaries, infusing an unparalleled global influence into the world of cocktails. With a rich tapestry of international flavors and techniques, the versatility of rosehip has inspired the creation of an impressive repertoire of fifty exquisite cocktails, each with its unique international flair and cultural significance. From the opulent splendor of the French Kir Royale to the tangy zest of the Canadian Bloody Caesar, the aromatic charm of the Russian White Russian to the vibrant sophistication of the Italian Bellini, and the boldness of the Scottish Rob Roy to the classic American Sidecar, each of these cocktails encapsulates the essence of its cultural heritage while celebrating the fusion of flavors that only rosehip can bring. Join us on a journey through this captivating array of fifty rosehip cocktails, where the spirit of global mixology converges to create an unforgettable sensory experience.

1. Rosehip Martini Recipe (United States)

The Rosehip Martini pays homage to the vibrant and tangy flavors of the rosehip fruit, popular for its historical significance and its contemporary appeal in the culinary and mixology scene. Inspired by the rich tradition of utilizing botanical ingredients in drinks, the Rosehip Martini emerged as a fusion of classic mixology techniques and innovative flavor combinations, capturing the essence of the modern cocktail renaissance. This elegant and refreshing martini embodies the spirit of creativity and craftsmanship, offering a delightful sensory experience that is both timeless and contemporary, just like the rosehips that inspired it. Enjoy the Rosehip Martini as a testament to the enduring legacy of the ever-evolving cocktail culture in the United States.

Ingredients:

- 2 ounces rosehip-infused vodka
- 1/2 ounce dry vermouth
- 1/2 ounce simple syrup
- Ice cubes
- Fresh rosehips or lemon twist, for garnish

Instructions:

1. To infuse the vodka, add dried rosehips to a bottle of vodka and let it sit for 3-5 days, allowing the flavors to meld.
2. In a mixing glass, combine the rosehip-infused vodka, dry vermouth, and simple syrup.
3. Fill the mixing glass with ice cubes and stir the ingredients until well-chilled.
4. Strain the mixture into a chilled martini glass.
5. Garnish the Rosehip Martini with fresh rosehips or a twist of lemon for an elegant presentation.
6. Serve and enjoy this delightful and sophisticated cocktail.

2. Rosehip Margarita (Mexico)

The Rosehip Margarita is a tribute to the vibrant and zesty flavors of traditional Mexican cuisine, where the art of mixing bold flavors with fresh ingredients is celebrated. Drawing inspiration from the cultural heritage of Mexico, the Rosehip Margarita encapsulates the essence of innovation and tradition, infusing the classic margarita with the tangy and floral essence of the rosehip. This contemporary twist on a beloved Mexican cocktail embodies the spirit of culinary exploration and pays homage to the rich legacy of Mexican flavors, inviting enthusiasts to savor the fusion of time-honored tradition and modern mixology. Enjoy the Rosehip Margarita as a toast to the enduring charm and diversity of Mexican culinary heritage.

Ingredients:

- 2 ounces tequila
- 1 ounce rosehip syrup
- 1 ounce freshly squeezed lime juice
- 1/2 ounce triple sec or Cointreau
- Rose petals and lime wedge, for garnish
- Ice cubes

Instructions:

1. Rim a margarita glass with salt, if desired, by running a lime wedge around the rim and dipping it into salt.
2. In a shaker, combine tequila, rosehip syrup, lime juice, and triple sec or Cointreau.
3. Add ice cubes to the shaker and shake vigorously for about 15-20 seconds.
4. Strain the mixture into the prepared margarita glass filled with ice.
5. Garnish the Rosehip Margarita with fresh rose petals and a lime wedge for an exquisite presentation.
6. Serve and enjoy this delightful and unique Mexican-inspired cocktail.

3. Rosehip Paloma (Mexico)

The Rosehip Paloma is a celebration of the lively and invigorating flavors of Mexico, where the art of blending fresh ingredients with authentic spirits is revered. Inspired by the rich tapestry of Mexican culture, the Rosehip Paloma embodies the spirit of innovation and tradition, infusing the classic Paloma with the tangy and floral essence of the rosehip. This contemporary rendition of a beloved Mexican cocktail encapsulates the essence of culinary exploration and pays homage to the vibrant legacy of Mexican flavors, inviting aficionados to indulge in the harmonious blend of time-honored tradition and modern mixology. Savor the Rosehip Paloma as a tribute to the enduring vibrancy and diversity of Mexican culinary heritage.

Ingredients:

- 2 ounces tequila
- 1/2 ounce rosehip syrup
- 2 ounces fresh grapefruit juice
- 1/2 ounce fresh lime juice
- Club soda
- Grapefruit wedge and rose petals, for garnish
- Ice cubes

Instructions:

1. Rim a highball glass with salt by running a grapefruit or lime wedge around the rim and dipping it into salt.
2. Fill the glass with ice cubes.
3. In a shaker, combine tequila, rosehip syrup, grapefruit juice, and lime juice.
4. Shake well for about 15-20 seconds.
5. Strain the mixture into the prepared highball glass over ice.
6. Top off with club soda.
7. Garnish the Rosehip Paloma with a grapefruit wedge and a sprinkle of rose petals for an elegant presentation.
8. Serve and enjoy this refreshing and vibrant Mexican-inspired cocktail.

4. Rosehip Michelada (Mexico)

The Rosehip Michelada is a tribute to the bold and spirited flavors of Mexico, where the art of concocting refreshing beverages with local ingredients is celebrated. Inspired by the rich cultural heritage of Mexico, the Rosehip Michelada captures the essence of innovation and tradition, infusing the classic Michelada with the tangy and floral essence of the rosehip. This contemporary twist on a cherished Mexican beer cocktail embodies the spirit of culinary adventure and pays homage to the vibrant legacy of Mexican flavors, inviting enthusiasts to relish the harmonious fusion of age-old tradition and modern mixology. Indulge in the Rosehip Michelada as a toast to the enduring vivacity and diversity of Mexican culinary heritage.

Ingredients:

- 1 chilled bottle of light Mexican beer
- 2 ounces tomato juice
- 1 ounce freshly squeezed lime juice
- 1/2 ounce rosehip syrup
- 3 dashes hot sauce (such as Tabasco)
- Tajin or salt, for rimming the glass
- Lime wedges and rose petals, for garnish
- Ice cubes

Instructions:

1. Rim a beer mug or glass with Tajin or salt by running a lime wedge around the rim and dipping it into the seasoning.
2. Fill the glass with ice cubes.
3. In a separate mixing glass, combine tomato juice, lime juice, rosehip syrup, and hot sauce.
4. Pour the mixture into the prepared beer mug or glass.
5. Slowly pour the chilled Mexican beer into the glass to combine with the mixture.
6. Garnish the Rosehip Michelada with lime wedges and a sprinkle of rose petals for a delightful presentation.
7. Serve and enjoy this invigorating and flavorful Mexican-inspired beer cocktail.

5. Rosehip Sangria (Spain)

The Rosehip Sangria is an ode to the lively and spirited flavors of Spain, where the art of crafting vibrant beverages with a medley of fruits and wine is treasured. Inspired by the rich cultural tapestry of Spain, the Rosehip Sangria captures the essence of tradition and innovation, infusing the classic Sangria with the tangy and floral essence of the rosehip. This contemporary adaptation of a beloved Spanish wine cocktail embodies the spirit of culinary exploration and pays homage to the vivacious legacy of Spanish flavors, inviting enthusiasts to revel in the harmonious blend of timeless tradition and modern mixology. Delight in the Rosehip Sangria as a tribute to the enduring charm and diversity of Spanish culinary heritage.

Ingredients:

- 1 bottle of red wine (750 ml)
- 1/2 cup rosehip syrup
- 1/4 cup brandy
- 1 cup sparkling water
- 1 orange, thinly sliced
- 1 lemon, thinly sliced
- 1 apple, thinly sliced
- Fresh rosehips, for garnish
- Ice cubes

Instructions:

1. In a large pitcher, combine red wine, rosehip syrup, and brandy.
2. Add the thinly sliced orange, lemon, and apple to the pitcher.
3. Stir the mixture gently to combine the flavors.
4. Refrigerate the sangria for at least 2 hours or until well-chilled.
5. Just before serving, add the sparkling water to the sangria and stir gently.
6. Fill glasses with ice cubes and pour the Rosehip Sangria over the ice.
7. Garnish each glass with fresh rosehips for a beautiful presentation.
8. Serve and enjoy this delightful and refreshing Spanish-inspired wine cocktail.

6. Rosehip Cava Cocktail (Spain)

The Rosehip Cava Cocktail from Spain embodies the country's rich cultural heritage and its love for vibrant, effervescent beverages. With a history steeped in tradition and a commitment to innovation, Spain has long been known for its festive and convivial spirit. Drawing inspiration from the captivating essence of Spanish celebrations, the Rosehip Cava Cocktail pays homage to the country's passion for creating memorable libations that combine the finest ingredients with a touch of sophistication. This contemporary blend, featuring the essence of the rosehip, captures the heart and soul of Spain, inviting enthusiasts to savor the lively fusion of tradition and modern mixology that is emblematic of the Spanish way of life.

Ingredients:

- 1 ounce rosehip syrup
- 4 ounces chilled Cava (Spanish sparkling wine)
- Fresh rose petals, for garnish
- Ice cubes

Instructions:

1. Pour the rosehip syrup into a Champagne flute or a wine glass.
2. Slowly add the chilled Cava to the glass, allowing it to mix gently with the rosehip syrup.
3. Drop a few ice cubes into the glass to maintain a refreshing chill.
4. Garnish the Rosehip Cava Cocktail with fresh rose petals for an elegant and aromatic touch.
5. Serve and enjoy this exquisite and bubbly Spanish-inspired cocktail, an ode to the enchanting flavors of Spain.

7. Rosehip Agua de Valencia (Spain)

Rosehip Agua de Valencia, a delightful Spanish cocktail, combines the vibrant flavors of the renowned Valencian orange with the floral essence of rosehip, offering a refreshing and invigorating experience. This delightful concoction pays homage to the lively and convivial spirit of the Valencian region, celebrated for its rich cultural heritage and its dedication to crafting exquisite libations that capture the essence of the land.

To prepare the Rosehip Agua de Valencia, follow the recipe below:

Ingredients:

- 1 cup freshly squeezed Valencian orange juice
- 1/4 cup rosehip syrup
- 1 cup chilled cava (Spanish sparkling wine)
- 1/4 cup vodka
- Ice cubes
- Fresh orange slices and rose petals, for garnish

Instructions:

1. In a pitcher, combine the freshly squeezed Valencian orange juice and rosehip syrup.
2. Slowly pour in the chilled cava and vodka, gently stirring the mixture to blend the flavors.
3. Fill glasses with ice cubes.
4. Pour the Rosehip Agua de Valencia into the glasses.
5. Garnish each glass with fresh orange slices and a sprinkle of rose petals for a visually appealing presentation.
6. Serve and enjoy this enchanting and aromatic Spanish-inspired cocktail, an ode to the vibrant and flavorful essence of the Valencian region.

8. Rosehip Tinto de Verano (Spain)

Rosehip Tinto de Verano is a delightful Spanish cocktail that infuses the rich flavors of rosehip with the invigorating essence of a classic Tinto de Verano. This refreshing beverage pays homage to the vibrant and convivial spirit of Spain, known for its dedication to creating memorable libations that embody the essence of the country's culture and traditions.

To prepare the Rosehip Tinto de Verano, follow the recipe below:

Ingredients:

- 1/4 cup rosehip syrup
- 1 cup red wine
- 1/2 cup lemon-lime soda or sparkling water
- Ice cubes
- Fresh lemon slices or rose petals, for garnish

Instructions:

1. In a pitcher, combine the rosehip syrup and red wine.
2. Add the lemon-lime soda or sparkling water to the pitcher, gently stirring to incorporate the ingredients.
3. Fill glasses with ice cubes.
4. Pour the Rosehip Tinto de Verano into the glasses.
5. Garnish each glass with fresh lemon slices or a sprinkle of rose petals for an elegant presentation.
6. Serve and enjoy this delightful and invigorating Spanish-inspired cocktail, embodying the vibrant and effervescent spirit of Spain.

9. Rosehip Gin and Tonic with a Twist (United Kingdom)

The Rosehip Gin and Tonic from the United Kingdom is a celebration of the country's rich heritage and its deep-rooted love for the classic G&T. Inspired by the British passion for creativity and innovation, this unique rendition infuses the traditional Gin and Tonic with the tangy and floral essence of rosehip, creating an extraordinary cocktail experience that is both familiar and delightfully unexpected. This contemporary blend captures the essence of British sophistication and pays tribute to the country's longstanding appreciation for the art of mixology and the exploration of new and exciting flavors.

Ingredients:

- 2 ounces gin
- 1/2 ounce rosehip syrup
- 4 ounces tonic water
- 1 tablespoon fresh thyme leaves
- 1/4 teaspoon black peppercorns
- Ice cubes
- Fresh rosehips or thyme sprigs, for garnish

Instructions:

1. In a mixing glass, muddle the fresh thyme leaves and black peppercorns to release their flavors.
2. Add the gin and rosehip syrup to the mixing glass, stirring gently to combine the ingredients.
3. Fill a highball glass with ice cubes.
4. Strain the gin and rosehip mixture into the glass.
5. Top off with tonic water and stir lightly.
6. Garnish the Rosehip Gin and Tonic with fresh rosehips or a sprig of thyme for an elegant and aromatic touch.
7. Serve and enjoy this extraordinary and refreshing British-inspired cocktail, a testament to the innovative spirit of the United Kingdom's mixology scene.

10. Rosehip Pimm's Cup (United Kingdom)

Rosehip Pimm's Cup is a delightful British cocktail that infuses the beloved Pimm's No. 1 with the vibrant and tangy essence of rosehip, creating a refreshing and flavorful beverage that embodies the spirit of British conviviality and sophistication.

To prepare the Rosehip Pimm's Cup, follow the recipe below:

Ingredients:

- 2 ounces Pimm's No. 1
- 1/2 ounce rosehip syrup
- 3 ounces lemon-lime soda
- Fresh cucumber slices
- Fresh strawberries, sliced
- Fresh mint leaves
- Fresh orange slices
- Ice cubes

Instructions:

1. In a Pimm's Cup glass, combine the Pimm's No. 1 and rosehip syrup.
2. Add a handful of ice cubes to the glass.
3. Layer the glass with fresh cucumber slices, sliced strawberries, and mint leaves.
4. Top off with lemon-lime soda.
5. Stir gently to combine the ingredients.
6. Garnish with fresh orange slices and a sprig of mint for an enticing presentation.
7. Serve and enjoy this delightful and vibrant British-inspired cocktail, capturing the essence of British tradition and the joy of shared moments among friends and family.

11. Rosehip Shandy (United Kingdom)

Rosehip Shandy is a refreshing British cocktail that combines the crisp and effervescent qualities of beer with the tangy and floral essence of rosehip, offering a delightful and invigorating beverage perfect for leisurely gatherings and social occasions.

To prepare the Rosehip Shandy, follow the recipe below:

Ingredients:

- 6 ounces chilled lager beer
- 2 ounces rosehip syrup
- 1 ounce fresh lemon juice
- Lemon slices for garnish
- Ice cubes

Instructions:

1. In a shaker, combine the rosehip syrup and fresh lemon juice.
2. Fill a glass with ice cubes.
3. Pour the chilled lager beer into the glass.
4. Slowly add the rosehip and lemon mixture to the beer, stirring gently to combine the flavors.
5. Garnish the Rosehip Shandy with fresh lemon slices for an appealing presentation.
6. Serve and enjoy this invigorating and crisp British-inspired cocktail, embodying the spirit of camaraderie and relaxation that defines the essence of British social culture.

12. Rosehip Hot Toddy (United Kingdom)

Rosehip Hot Toddy is a comforting and aromatic British cocktail, perfect for warming up during chilly evenings. Infusing the classic Hot Toddy with the tangy sweetness of rosehip creates a delightful blend that embodies the British appreciation for cozy moments and soothing libations.

To prepare the Rosehip Hot Toddy, follow the recipe below:

Ingredients:

- 2 ounces whiskey
- 1 tablespoon rosehip syrup
- 1/2 ounce fresh lemon juice
- 1 cup hot water
- Lemon slice studded with cloves, for garnish
- Cinnamon stick, for garnish
- Honey, to taste (optional)

Instructions:

1. In a heat-resistant glass or mug, combine the whiskey, rosehip syrup, and fresh lemon juice.
2. Pour in the hot water and stir gently to combine the ingredients.
3. Add honey to taste, if desired, and stir until dissolved.
4. Garnish the Rosehip Hot Toddy with a lemon slice studded with cloves and a cinnamon stick for added warmth and aroma.
5. Sip and savor this comforting and soothing British-inspired cocktail, reveling in the delightful blend of flavors and the cozy embrace of a well-made Hot Toddy.

13. Rosehip Mulled Wine (United Kingdom)

Rosehip Mulled Wine is a delightful British beverage that combines the rich and aromatic flavors of traditional mulled wine with the tangy sweetness of rosehip, creating a comforting and festive drink that embodies the essence of wintertime gatherings and holiday cheer.

To prepare the Rosehip Mulled Wine, follow the recipe below:

Ingredients:

- 1 bottle of red wine (750 ml)
- 1/4 cup rosehip syrup
- 1 orange, sliced
- 8-10 whole cloves
- 2 cinnamon sticks
- 1/4 cup honey or sweetener of choice (optional)
- 1/4 cup brandy (optional for added warmth)
- Star anise, for garnish (optional)

Instructions:

1. In a large saucepan, combine the red wine and rosehip syrup over low heat.
2. Add the sliced orange, cloves, and cinnamon sticks to the saucepan, stirring gently.
3. Allow the mixture to simmer gently for 20-30 minutes, ensuring it doesn't come to a boil.
4. Optionally, add honey or sweetener to taste, and brandy for added warmth and richness.
5. Once the flavors have melded, remove the saucepan from the heat.
6. Strain the mulled wine into mugs or heat-resistant glasses.
7. Garnish each glass with a star anise for an added touch of festive flair.
8. Serve and enjoy this comforting and aromatic British-inspired beverage, reveling in the delightful blend of flavors and the warmth it brings to festive gatherings and cozy evenings.

14. Rosehip Negroni (Italy)

This Rosehip Negroni offers a delightful twist on the classic Italian cocktail, infusing it with the tangy sweetness of rosehip, adding a layer of complexity and a subtle floral note to this beloved drink. Enjoy this sophisticated and balanced cocktail, perfect for sipping and savoring.

Ingredients:

- 1 ounce gin
- 1 ounce Campari
- 1 ounce sweet vermouth
- 1/2 ounce rosehip syrup
- Orange peel, for garnish
- Ice cubes

Instructions:

1. Fill a mixing glass with ice cubes.
2. Add the gin, Campari, sweet vermouth, and rosehip syrup to the mixing glass.
3. Stir the mixture well for about 30 seconds to chill and properly dilute the drink.
4. Strain the mixture into a chilled rocks glass filled with fresh ice.
5. Express the oils from an orange peel over the cocktail by squeezing it over the glass.
6. Garnish the Rosehip Negroni with the orange peel and serve immediately.

15. Rosehip Aperol Spritz (Italy)

The Rosehip Aperol Spritz pays tribute to the iconic Aperol Spritz, a beloved Italian cocktail celebrated for its vibrant and refreshing flavors. Drawing inspiration from the zest for life that defines Italian culture, this innovative variation infuses the classic Aperol Spritz with the tangy and floral essence of rosehip, creating a delightful libation that captures the essence of Italian conviviality and the art of savoring the moment. Embodying the spirit of shared laughter and cherished gatherings, the Rosehip Aperol Spritz offers a refreshing and aromatic experience that is both timeless and evocative of the enchanting Italian lifestyle.

Ingredients:

- 3 ounces Prosecco
- 2 ounces Aperol
- 1 ounce rosehip syrup
- Splash of soda water
- Orange slice, for garnish
- Ice cubes

Instructions:

1. Fill a large wine glass with ice cubes.
2. Add the Prosecco, Aperol, and rosehip syrup to the glass.
3. Stir gently to combine the ingredients.
4. Top off the mixture with a splash of soda water.
5. Garnish the Rosehip Aperol Spritz with an orange slice for a vibrant and citrusy touch.
6. Serve and enjoy this invigorating and flavorful Italian-inspired cocktail, a testament to the joy of shared moments and the zest for life that defines the Italian spirit.

16. Rosehip Bellini (Italy)

The Rosehip Bellini is a celebration of Italian sophistication and the art of crafting elegant and refreshing cocktails. Inspired by the iconic Bellini, renowned for its timeless appeal and luscious flavors, this unique variation infuses the classic cocktail with the tangy and floral essence of rosehip, capturing the essence of Italian romance and culinary finesse. The Rosehip Bellini embodies the spirit of elegance and celebration, inviting enthusiasts to savor the enchanting fusion of tradition and innovation that defines the Italian culinary heritage.

Ingredients:

- 2 ounces peach puree or peach nectar
- 1/2 ounce rosehip syrup
- Chilled Prosecco
- Fresh rose petals, for garnish

Instructions:

1. In a chilled champagne flute, pour the peach puree or peach nectar.
2. Add the rosehip syrup to the flute.
3. Slowly fill the flute with chilled Prosecco.
4. Gently stir the mixture to combine the flavors.
5. Garnish the Rosehip Bellini with fresh rose petals for an exquisite and aromatic presentation.
6. Serve and enjoy this elegant and delightful Italian-inspired cocktail, evoking the enchanting spirit of romance and the timeless allure of Italian culinary craftsmanship.

17. Rosehip Campari Soda (Italy)

The Rosehip Campari Soda is a tribute to the iconic Italian aperitif culture, renowned for its vibrant and bitter-sweet flavors. Inspired by the zest for life that defines Italian gatherings, this refreshing concoction infuses the classic Campari Soda with the tangy and floral essence of rosehip, creating a delightful libation that embodies the spirit of Italian conviviality and the appreciation of refreshing aperitifs. The Rosehip Campari Soda encapsulates the essence of shared laughter and cherished moments, offering a revitalizing and aromatic experience that is both invigorating and reminiscent of the enchanting Italian lifestyle.

Ingredients:

- 2 ounces Campari
- 1 ounce rosehip syrup
- Soda water
- Fresh orange slice, for garnish
- Ice cubes

Instructions:

1. Fill a highball glass with ice cubes.
2. Pour the Campari and rosehip syrup into the glass.
3. Top off the glass with soda water.
4. Stir gently to mix the ingredients.
5. Garnish the Rosehip Campari Soda with a fresh orange slice for a vibrant and citrusy touch.
6. Serve and enjoy this invigorating and flavorful Italian-inspired aperitif, celebrating the spirit of shared moments and the zest for life that characterizes the Italian way of living.

18. Rosehip Sgroppino (Italy)

The Rosehip Sgroppino is a tribute to the rich culinary traditions of Italy, renowned for its indulgent and refreshing palate cleansers. Drawing inspiration from the classic Sgroppino, celebrated for its luxurious and invigorating flavors, this innovative rendition infuses the traditional cocktail with the tangy and floral essence of rosehip, creating a delightful libation that embodies the spirit of Italian hospitality and the art of savoring life's pleasures. The Rosehip Sgroppino captures the essence of sophistication and indulgence, inviting enthusiasts to relish the enchanting blend of tradition and innovation that defines the Italian culinary heritage.

Ingredients:

- 1 scoop lemon sorbet
- 1 ounce vodka
- 1/2 ounce rosehip syrup
- Chilled Prosecco
- Fresh mint leaves, for garnish

Instructions:

1. In a chilled champagne flute, place a scoop of lemon sorbet.
2. Add the vodka and rosehip syrup to the flute.
3. Slowly pour the chilled Prosecco into the flute.
4. Gently stir the mixture to combine the flavors.
5. Garnish the Rosehip Sgroppino with fresh mint leaves for a refreshing and aromatic touch.
6. Serve and enjoy this luxurious and delightful Italian-inspired cocktail, celebrating the spirit of indulgence and the joy of savoring life's exquisite pleasures.

19. Rosehip Limoncello (Italy)

Rosehip Limoncello pays homage to the illustrious Italian tradition of crafting exquisite liqueurs, celebrated for their vibrant and citrusy flavors. Drawing inspiration from the renowned Limoncello, known for its zesty and refreshing taste, this unique fusion infuses the classic liqueur with the tangy sweetness of rosehip, creating a delightful libation that captures the essence of Italian zest for life and culinary finesse. Rosehip Limoncello embodies the spirit of indulgence and celebration, inviting enthusiasts to savor the enchanting blend of tradition and innovation that defines the Italian liqueur heritage.

Ingredients:

- 6 organic lemons
- 2 cups vodka
- 1 cup rosehip syrup
- 2 cups water
- 1 1/2 cups granulated sugar

Instructions:

1. Wash the lemons thoroughly and peel them, ensuring no white pith is included.
2. Place the lemon peels in a large glass jar and pour the vodka over the peels.
3. Seal the jar and let it sit for at least 5 days in a cool, dark place.
4. In a saucepan, combine the rosehip syrup, water, and sugar, stirring over low heat until the sugar has dissolved.
5. Let the syrup cool completely.
6. Strain the infused vodka into a large bowl and discard the lemon peels.
7. Add the cooled rosehip syrup to the infused vodka, stirring to combine.
8. Transfer the mixture to a clean glass bottle and let it sit for at least 2 weeks in the refrigerator.
9. Serve the Rosehip Limoncello chilled in small liqueur glasses, savoring the vibrant and tangy flavors that encapsulate the essence of Italian zest and sophistication.

20. Rosehip Amaro (Italy)

Rosehip Amaro pays homage to the revered Italian tradition of crafting complex and herbaceous liqueurs, celebrated for their bitter-sweet and aromatic flavors. Inspired by the iconic Amaro, known for its rich and invigorating taste, this unique infusion infuses the classic liqueur with the tangy sweetness of rosehip, creating a delightful libation that embodies the spirit of Italian conviviality and the art of savoring flavors. Rosehip Amaro encapsulates the essence of indulgence and sophistication, inviting enthusiasts to relish the enchanting fusion of tradition and innovation that defines the Italian liqueur heritage.

Ingredients:

- 1 cup dried rosehips
- 2 cups vodka
- 1/2 cup water
- 1 cup granulated sugar
- 1 tablespoon dried orange peel
- 1 tablespoon dried lemon peel
- 1 tablespoon dried chamomile flowers
- 1 tablespoon dried thyme
- 1/2 teaspoon whole cloves
- 1 cinnamon stick
- 1 vanilla bean, split
- 1 star anise
- 1 cup simple syrup

Instructions:

1. In a large glass jar, combine the dried rosehips and vodka. Seal the jar and let it sit for at least 2 weeks in a cool, dark place, shaking occasionally.
2. In a saucepan, combine the water, sugar, dried orange peel, dried lemon peel, chamomile flowers, thyme, cloves, cinnamon stick, vanilla bean, and star anise. Bring the mixture to a boil, then reduce the heat and let it simmer for 15-20 minutes. Allow the mixture to cool completely.
3. Strain the infused vodka into a large bowl and discard the rosehips.
4. Add the cooled herb mixture and the simple syrup to the infused vodka, stirring to combine.
5. Transfer the mixture to a clean glass bottle and let it sit for at least 2 weeks in a cool, dark place.
6. Serve the Rosehip Amaro neat or on the rocks, savoring the rich and complex flavors that embody the essence of Italian sophistication and culinary craftsmanship.

21. Rosehip Vermouth (Italy)

Rosehip Vermouth pays homage to the storied Italian tradition of crafting flavorful and aromatic fortified wines, celebrated for their rich and complex taste profiles. Inspired by the classic Vermouth, renowned for its herbal and botanical nuances, this innovative adaptation infuses the traditional wine with the tangy and floral essence of rosehip, creating a delightful libation that captures the essence of Italian artistry and the enjoyment of sophisticated beverages. Rosehip Vermouth embodies the spirit of indulgence and celebration, inviting enthusiasts to relish the enchanting blend of tradition and innovation that defines the Italian winemaking heritage.

Ingredients:

- 1 bottle of dry white wine (750 ml)
- 1/4 cup rosehip syrup
- 1/4 cup vodka
- 2 tablespoons dried rosehips
- 1 tablespoon dried orange peel
- 1 tablespoon dried lemon peel
- 1 tablespoon dried chamomile flowers
- 1 cinnamon stick
- 1 vanilla bean, split
- 4-5 whole cloves
- 1/4 cup honey or sweetener of choice
- 1/2 cup water

Instructions:

1. In a large glass jar, combine the white wine and rosehip syrup. Add the vodka and stir gently to combine.
2. Add the dried rosehips, dried orange peel, dried lemon peel, chamomile flowers, cinnamon stick, vanilla bean, and cloves to the jar.
3. Seal the jar and let it sit for at least 2 weeks in a cool, dark place, shaking occasionally.
4. In a saucepan, combine the honey and water, stirring over low heat until the honey has dissolved.
5. Let the honey syrup cool completely.
6. Strain the infused wine into a large bowl, removing the herbs and spices.
7. Add the honey syrup to the infused wine, stirring to combine.
8. Transfer the Rosehip Vermouth to a clean glass bottle and let it sit for an additional 1-2 weeks to allow the flavors to meld.
9. Serve the Rosehip Vermouth chilled or on the rocks, savoring the nuanced and delightful flavors that epitomize the essence of Italian sophistication and the art of wine-making.

22. Rosehip Sazerac (United States)

The Rosehip Sazerac is a tribute to the rich history of American mixology and the timeless tradition of crafting bold and flavorful cocktails. Inspired by the classic Sazerac, celebrated for its robust and aromatic qualities, this innovative adaptation infuses the traditional cocktail with the tangy sweetness of rosehip, creating a delightful libation that embodies the spirit of American craftsmanship and the art of savoring meticulously curated drinks. The Rosehip Sazerac encapsulates the essence of refinement and heritage, inviting enthusiasts to relish the enchanting blend of tradition and innovation that defines the American cocktail culture.

Ingredients:

- 2 ounces rye whiskey
- 1/4 ounce rosehip syrup
- 3 dashes Peychaud's Bitters
- Absinthe rinse
- Lemon peel, for garnish
- Ice cubes

Instructions:

1. Rinse a chilled Old Fashioned glass with absinthe, discarding the excess.
2. In a separate mixing glass, combine the rye whiskey, rosehip syrup, and Peychaud's Bitters.
3. Fill the mixing glass with ice cubes and stir the mixture until well-chilled.
4. Strain the mixture into the prepared Old Fashioned glass.
5. Express the oils from a lemon peel over the cocktail by squeezing it over the glass.
6. Garnish the Rosehip Sazerac with the lemon peel and serve immediately.

Enjoy this sophisticated and flavorful American-inspired cocktail, celebrating the country's rich cocktail heritage and the vibrant flavors that epitomize the American spirit of innovation and creativity.

23. Rosehip Old Fashioned (United States)

The Rosehip Old Fashioned is a tribute to the storied tradition of American mixology and the timeless art of crafting sophisticated and flavorful cocktails. Inspired by the classic Old Fashioned, celebrated for its timeless appeal and robust flavors, this innovative adaptation infuses the traditional cocktail with the tangy sweetness of rosehip, creating a delightful libation that embodies the spirit of American craftsmanship and the appreciation of well-balanced drinks. The Rosehip Old Fashioned encapsulates the essence of refinement and heritage, inviting enthusiasts to relish the enchanting blend of tradition and innovation that defines the American cocktail culture.

Ingredients:

- 2 ounces bourbon or rye whiskey
- 1/2 ounce rosehip syrup
- 2 dashes Angostura Bitters
- Orange peel, for garnish
- Luxardo cherry, for garnish
- Ice cubes

Instructions:

1. In an Old Fashioned glass, combine the rosehip syrup and Angostura Bitters.
2. Fill the glass with ice cubes.
3. Pour the bourbon or rye whiskey over the ice and stir gently to combine the ingredients.
4. Express the oils from an orange peel over the cocktail by squeezing it over the glass.
5. Garnish the Rosehip Old Fashioned with the orange peel and a Luxardo cherry for an added touch of sweetness.
6. Serve and enjoy this sophisticated and flavorful American-inspired cocktail, savoring the rich and complex flavors that embody the essence of American innovation and the art of mixology.

24. Rosehip Manhattan (United States)

The Rosehip Manhattan pays homage to the rich history of American mixology and the timeless tradition of crafting bold and sophisticated cocktails. Inspired by the classic Manhattan, celebrated for its balanced and flavorful character, this unique adaptation infuses the traditional cocktail with the tangy sweetness of rosehip, creating a delightful libation that captures the spirit of American craftsmanship and the art of savoring meticulously crafted drinks. The Rosehip Manhattan embodies the essence of refinement and heritage, inviting enthusiasts to relish the enchanting fusion of tradition and innovation that defines the American cocktail culture.

Ingredients:

- 2 ounces rye whiskey
- 1 ounce sweet vermouth
- 1/2 ounce rosehip syrup
- 2 dashes Angostura Bitters
- Maraschino cherry, for garnish
- Ice cubes

Instructions:

1. In a mixing glass, combine the rye whiskey, sweet vermouth, rosehip syrup, and Angostura Bitters.
2. Fill the mixing glass with ice cubes and stir the mixture until well-chilled.
3. Strain the mixture into a chilled cocktail glass.
4. Drop a Maraschino cherry into the glass for garnish.
5. Serve and enjoy this sophisticated and flavorful American-inspired cocktail, celebrating the rich history and dynamic flavors that epitomize the American spirit of innovation and creativity in mixology.

25. Rosehip Boulevardier (United States)

The Rosehip Boulevardier is a tribute to the rich legacy of American mixology and the enduring tradition of crafting robust and complex cocktails. Drawing inspiration from the classic Boulevardier, celebrated for its bold and bittersweet flavors, this inventive adaptation infuses the traditional cocktail with the tangy sweetness of rosehip, creating a delightful libation that embodies the spirit of American craftsmanship and the appreciation of well-balanced libations. The Rosehip Boulevardier encapsulates the essence of sophistication and heritage, inviting enthusiasts to savor the enchanting fusion of tradition and innovation that defines the American cocktail culture.

Ingredients:

- 1 1/2 ounces bourbon
- 1 ounce Campari
- 1 ounce sweet vermouth
- 1/2 ounce rosehip syrup
- Orange peel, for garnish
- Ice cubes

Instructions:

1. In a mixing glass, combine the bourbon, Campari, sweet vermouth, and rosehip syrup.
2. Fill the mixing glass with ice cubes and stir the mixture until well-chilled.
3. Strain the mixture into a chilled rocks glass filled with ice.
4. Express the oils from an orange peel over the cocktail by squeezing it over the glass.
5. Garnish the Rosehip Boulevardier with the orange peel and serve immediately.

Enjoy this sophisticated and flavorful American-inspired cocktail, celebrating the country's rich cocktail heritage and the vibrant flavors that epitomize the American spirit of innovation and creativity in mixology.

26. Rosehip Whiskey Sour (United States)

The Rosehip Whiskey Sour is a tribute to the rich history of American mixology and the enduring tradition of crafting balanced and refreshing cocktails. Inspired by the classic Whiskey Sour, celebrated for its timeless appeal and harmonious flavors, this innovative adaptation infuses the traditional cocktail with the tangy sweetness of rosehip, creating a delightful libation that embodies the spirit of American craftsmanship and the appreciation of well-crafted libations. The Rosehip Whiskey Sour encapsulates the essence of vibrancy and heritage, inviting enthusiasts to savor the enchanting fusion of tradition and innovation that defines the American cocktail culture.

Ingredients:

- 2 ounces whiskey
- 3/4 ounce fresh lemon juice
- 1/2 ounce rosehip syrup
- 1/2 ounce simple syrup
- Maraschino cherry and orange slice, for garnish
- Ice cubes

Instructions:

1. In a shaker, combine the whiskey, fresh lemon juice, rosehip syrup, and simple syrup.
2. Fill the shaker with ice cubes and shake vigorously for about 15 seconds.
3. Strain the mixture into a rocks glass filled with ice.
4. Garnish the Rosehip Whiskey Sour with a Maraschino cherry and an orange slice for a vibrant and citrusy touch.
5. Serve and enjoy this invigorating and flavorful American-inspired cocktail, celebrating the rich history and dynamic flavors that epitomize the American spirit of innovation and creativity in mixology.

27. Rosehip Mint Julep (United States)

The Rosehip Mint Julep pays homage to the esteemed heritage of American mixology and the timeless tradition of crafting refreshing and aromatic cocktails. Drawing inspiration from the classic Mint Julep, renowned for its invigorating and herbaceous flavors, this unique adaptation infuses the traditional cocktail with the tangy sweetness of rosehip, creating a delightful libation that captures the spirit of American craftsmanship and the art of savoring meticulously curated drinks. The Rosehip Mint Julep embodies the essence of vibrancy and heritage, inviting enthusiasts to relish the enchanting fusion of tradition and innovation that defines the American cocktail culture.

Ingredients:

- 2 ounces bourbon
- 1/2 ounce rosehip syrup
- 4-5 fresh mint leaves
- Crushed ice
- Fresh mint sprig, for garnish

Instructions:

1. In a Julep cup or rocks glass, muddle the fresh mint leaves with the rosehip syrup.
2. Fill the glass with crushed ice.
3. Pour the bourbon over the ice and stir gently to combine the ingredients.
4. Garnish the Rosehip Mint Julep with a fresh mint sprig for a vibrant and aromatic touch.
5. Serve and enjoy this invigorating and flavorful American-inspired cocktail, celebrating the country's rich cocktail heritage and the vibrant flavors that epitomize the American spirit of innovation and creativity in mixology.

28. Rosehip Hot Buttered Rum (United States)

The Rosehip Hot Buttered Rum is a tribute to the rich history of American mixology and the enduring tradition of crafting comforting and flavorful warm beverages. Inspired by the classic Hot Buttered Rum, celebrated for its rich and indulgent flavors, this innovative adaptation infuses the traditional drink with the tangy sweetness of rosehip, creating a delightful libation that embodies the spirit of American craftsmanship and the art of savoring soul-warming libations. The Rosehip Hot Buttered Rum encapsulates the essence of comfort and heritage, inviting enthusiasts to relish the enchanting fusion of tradition and innovation that defines the American beverage culture.

Ingredients:

- 2 ounces dark rum
- 1/2 ounce rosehip syrup
- 1 tablespoon unsalted butter
- 1 tablespoon brown sugar
- Pinch of ground cinnamon
- Pinch of ground nutmeg
- Hot water
- Cinnamon stick, for garnish

Instructions:

1. In a heatproof glass, combine the dark rum and rosehip syrup.
2. In a separate mixing bowl, cream together the unsalted butter, brown sugar, ground cinnamon, and ground nutmeg.
3. Spoon the butter mixture into the glass with the rum and rosehip syrup.
4. Fill the glass with hot water and stir gently to melt the butter mixture.
5. Garnish the Rosehip Hot Buttered Rum with a cinnamon stick for a flavorful and aromatic touch.
6. Serve and enjoy this comforting and delightful American-inspired beverage, celebrating the rich history and heartwarming flavors that epitomize the spirit of American hospitality and beverage craftsmanship.

29. Rosehip Irish Coffee (Ireland)

The Rosehip Irish Coffee is a tribute to the rich tradition of Irish hospitality and the enduring legacy of crafting warm and invigorating beverages. Inspired by the classic Irish Coffee, celebrated for its comforting and indulgent qualities, this innovative adaptation infuses the traditional drink with the tangy sweetness of rosehip, creating a delightful libation that embodies the spirit of Irish conviviality and the art of savoring soul-warming libations. The Rosehip Irish Coffee encapsulates the essence of comfort and heritage, inviting enthusiasts to savor the enchanting fusion of tradition and innovation that defines the Irish beverage culture.

Ingredients:

- 1 1/2 ounces Irish whiskey
- 1/2 ounce rosehip syrup
- 5-6 ounces hot brewed coffee
- Freshly whipped cream
- Ground cinnamon, for garnish

Instructions:

1. In a heatproof glass, combine the Irish whiskey and rosehip syrup.
2. Pour the hot brewed coffee over the whiskey mixture and stir gently to combine.
3. Top the Rosehip Irish Coffee with a generous dollop of freshly whipped cream.
4. Sprinkle a dash of ground cinnamon over the whipped cream for an aromatic and flavorful touch.
5. Serve and enjoy this comforting and delightful Irish-inspired beverage, celebrating the rich history and warm flavors that epitomize the heartwarming spirit of Irish hospitality and beverage craftsmanship.

30. Rosehip Black Velvet (Ireland)

The Rosehip Black Velvet is a tribute to the rich tradition of Irish conviviality and the enduring legacy of crafting luxurious and effervescent cocktails. Drawing inspiration from the classic Black Velvet, renowned for its elegant and opulent qualities, this unique adaptation infuses the traditional cocktail with the tangy sweetness of rosehip, creating a delightful libation that captures the spirit of Irish hospitality and the art of savoring sophisticated libations.

The Rosehip Black Velvet encapsulates the essence of refinement and heritage, inviting enthusiasts to relish the enchanting fusion of tradition and innovation that defines the Irish beverage culture.

Ingredients:

- 3 ounces champagne or sparkling wine
- 3 ounces stout beer
- 1/2 ounce rosehip syrup
- Fresh blackberries, for garnish

Instructions:

1. In a champagne flute, pour the champagne or sparkling wine halfway.
2. Slowly pour the stout beer over the back of a spoon to create a layered effect on top of the champagne.
3. Drizzle the rosehip syrup over the cocktail.
4. Garnish the Rosehip Black Velvet with fresh blackberries for a vibrant and fruity touch.
5. Serve and enjoy this sophisticated and flavorful Irish-inspired cocktail, celebrating the rich history and luxurious flavors that epitomize the spirit of Irish conviviality and beverage craftsmanship.

31. Rosehip Guinness Punch (Ireland)

The Rosehip Guinness Punch is a celebration of the rich Irish culinary heritage and the art of crafting robust and flavorful beverages. Inspired by the renowned Guinness Punch, celebrated for its hearty and invigorating qualities, this innovative adaptation infuses the traditional punch with the tangy sweetness of rosehip, creating a delightful libation that embodies the spirit of Irish conviviality and the appreciation of well-balanced libations. The Rosehip Guinness Punch encapsulates the essence of warmth and heritage, inviting enthusiasts to savor the enchanting fusion of tradition and innovation that defines the Irish beverage culture.

Ingredients:

- 12 ounces Guinness stout
- 1 ounce rosehip syrup
- 1/2 ounce fresh lime juice
- 1/2 ounce simple syrup
- Pinch of ground nutmeg
- Ice cubes
- Lime wheel, for garnish

Instructions:

1. In a cocktail shaker, combine the Guinness stout, rosehip syrup, fresh lime juice, simple syrup, and ground nutmeg.
2. Add ice cubes to the shaker and shake vigorously for about 10-15 seconds.
3. Strain the mixture into a highball glass filled with ice.
4. Garnish the Rosehip Guinness Punch with a lime wheel for a vibrant and citrusy touch.
5. Serve and enjoy this invigorating and flavorful Irish-inspired beverage, celebrating the rich history and dynamic flavors that epitomize the spirit of Irish conviviality and beverage craftsmanship.

32. Rosehip Baileys Irish Cream (Ireland)

The Rosehip Baileys Irish Cream is a tribute to the rich tradition of Irish indulgence and the enduring legacy of crafting creamy and luxurious liqueurs. Drawing inspiration from the classic Baileys Irish Cream, celebrated for its smooth and velvety texture, this unique adaptation infuses the traditional liqueur with the tangy sweetness of rosehip, creating a delightful libation that captures the spirit of Irish conviviality and the art of savoring rich and indulgent beverages.

The Rosehip Baileys Irish Cream encapsulates the essence of comfort and heritage, inviting enthusiasts to relish the enchanting fusion of tradition and innovation that defines the Irish liqueur culture.

Ingredients:

- 1 cup heavy cream
- 1 can (14 ounces) sweetened condensed milk
- 1 2/3 cups Irish whiskey
- 2 tablespoons rosehip syrup
- 1 teaspoon instant coffee granules
- 1 teaspoon vanilla extract
- 1/2 teaspoon almond extract
- 1/4 teaspoon cocoa powder

Instructions:

1. In a blender, combine the heavy cream, sweetened condensed milk, Irish whiskey, rosehip syrup, instant coffee granules, vanilla extract, almond extract, and cocoa powder.
2. Blend the mixture on high speed for about 30 seconds to 1 minute, ensuring that all the ingredients are fully combined and the mixture is smooth and creamy.
3. Strain the mixture through a fine-mesh sieve to remove any lumps or particles.
4. Pour the Rosehip Baileys Irish Cream into a clean glass bottle or jar with a tight-fitting lid.
5. Refrigerate the liqueur for at least 2 hours or until chilled and slightly thickened.
6. Serve the Rosehip Baileys Irish Cream over ice or incorporate it into various cocktails, savoring the rich and velvety flavors that epitomize the spirit of Irish indulgence and the art of liqueur craftsmanship.

33. Rosehip Jameson and Ginger (Ireland)

The Rosehip Jameson and Ginger is another celebration of the rich Irish culinary heritage and the art of crafting refreshing and vibrant cocktails. Inspired by the classic Jameson and Ginger, renowned for its invigorating and lively qualities, this unique adaptation infuses the traditional cocktail with the tangy sweetness of rosehip, creating a delightful libation that embodies the spirit of Irish conviviality and the appreciation of well-balanced libations.

The Rosehip Jameson and Ginger encapsulates the essence of vibrancy and heritage, inviting enthusiasts to relish the enchanting fusion of tradition and innovation that defines the Irish cocktail culture.

Recipe:

Rosehip Jameson and Ginger

Ingredients:

- 2 ounces Jameson Irish whiskey
- 4 ounces ginger ale
- 1/2 ounce rosehip syrup
- Lime wedge, for garnish
- Ice cubes

Instructions:

1. Fill a highball glass with ice cubes.
2. Pour the Jameson Irish whiskey over the ice.
3. Add the ginger ale to the glass and stir gently to combine the ingredients.
4. Drizzle the rosehip syrup over the cocktail.
5. Squeeze the juice from a lime wedge into the glass and drop the wedge in as a garnish.
6. Serve and enjoy this invigorating and flavorful Irish-inspired cocktail, celebrating the rich history and dynamic flavors that epitomize the spirit of Irish conviviality and beverage craftsmanship.

34. Rosehip Rusty Nail (Scotland)

The Rosehip Rusty Nail is a tribute to the rich Scottish tradition of whisky appreciation and the enduring legacy of crafting strong and sophisticated cocktails. Drawing inspiration from the classic Rusty Nail, celebrated for its bold and robust flavors, this unique adaptation infuses the traditional cocktail with the tangy sweetness of rosehip, creating a delightful libation that captures the spirit of Scottish craftsmanship and the art of savoring meticulously curated drinks.

The Rosehip Rusty Nail encapsulates the essence of refinement and heritage, inviting enthusiasts to relish the enchanting fusion of tradition and innovation that defines the Scottish cocktail culture.

Ingredients:

- 1 1/2 ounces Scotch whisky
- 1/2 ounce Drambuie
- 1/4 ounce rosehip syrup
- Lemon twist, for garnish
- Ice cubes

Instructions:

1. Fill a mixing glass with ice cubes.
2. Pour the Scotch whisky, Drambuie, and rosehip syrup over the ice.
3. Stir the mixture gently for about 30 seconds to combine the ingredients and chill the mixture.
4. Strain the mixture into a chilled rocks glass filled with fresh ice.
5. Express the oils from a lemon twist over the cocktail by squeezing it over the glass.
6. Garnish the Rosehip Rusty Nail with the lemon twist for a citrusy and aromatic touch.
7. Serve and enjoy this sophisticated and flavorful Scottish-inspired cocktail, celebrating the rich history and dynamic flavors that epitomize the spirit of Scottish refinement and beverage craftsmanship.

35. Rosehip Scotch Sour (Scotland)

The Rosehip Scotch Sour is a tribute to the rich Scottish tradition of whisky craftsmanship and the enduring legacy of crafting balanced and flavorful cocktails. Drawing inspiration from the classic Whisky Sour, renowned for its timeless appeal and harmonious flavors, this unique adaptation infuses the traditional cocktail with the tangy sweetness of rosehip, creating a delightful libation that captures the spirit of Scottish conviviality and the appreciation of well-crafted libations.

The Rosehip Scotch Sour encapsulates the essence of vibrancy and heritage, inviting enthusiasts to savor the enchanting fusion of tradition and innovation that defines the Scottish cocktail culture.

Ingredients:

- 2 ounces Scotch whisky
- 3/4 ounce fresh lemon juice
- 1/2 ounce rosehip syrup
- 1/4 ounce simple syrup
- 1 egg white
- Lemon twist, for garnish
- Ice cubes

Instructions:

1. In a shaker, combine the Scotch whisky, fresh lemon juice, rosehip syrup, simple syrup, and egg white.
2. Fill the shaker with ice cubes and shake vigorously for about 15-20 seconds to emulsify the egg white.
3. Strain the mixture into a chilled sour glass or rocks glass filled with ice.
4. Express the oils from a lemon twist over the cocktail by squeezing it over the glass.
5. Garnish the Rosehip Scotch Sour with the lemon twist for a vibrant and citrusy touch.
6. Serve and enjoy this invigorating and flavorful Scottish-inspired cocktail, celebrating the rich history and dynamic flavors that epitomize the spirit of Scottish conviviality and beverage craftsmanship.

36. Rosehip Rob Roy (Scotland)

The Rosehip Rob Roy is a tribute to the rich Scottish tradition of whisky appreciation and the enduring legacy of crafting elegant and sophisticated cocktails. Inspired by the classic Rob Roy, celebrated for its smooth and nuanced flavors, this unique adaptation infuses the traditional cocktail with the tangy sweetness of rosehip, creating a delightful libation that embodies the spirit of Scottish refinement and the appreciation of well-balanced libations.

The Rosehip Rob Roy encapsulates the essence of sophistication and heritage, inviting enthusiasts to savor the enchanting fusion of tradition and innovation that defines the Scottish cocktail culture.

Recipe:

Rosehip Rob Roy

Ingredients:

- 2 ounces Scotch whisky
- 1 ounce sweet vermouth
- 1/4 ounce rosehip syrup
- 2 dashes Angostura Bitters
- Maraschino cherry, for garnish
- Ice cubes

Instructions:

1. In a mixing glass, combine the Scotch whisky, sweet vermouth, rosehip syrup, and Angostura Bitters.
2. Fill the mixing glass with ice cubes and stir the mixture until well-chilled.
3. Strain the mixture into a chilled cocktail glass.
4. Drop a Maraschino cherry into the glass for garnish.
5. Serve and enjoy this sophisticated and flavorful Scottish-inspired cocktail, celebrating the rich history and nuanced flavors that epitomize the spirit of Scottish refinement and the art of cocktail craftsmanship.

37. Rosehip Blood and Sand (Scotland)

The Rosehip Blood and Sand is a celebration of the rich Scottish culinary heritage and the art of crafting bold and flavorful cocktails. Inspired by the classic Blood and Sand, renowned for its complex and harmonious flavors, this unique adaptation infuses the traditional cocktail with the tangy sweetness of rosehip, creating a delightful libation that captures the spirit of Scottish conviviality and the appreciation of well-balanced libations.

The Rosehip Blood and Sand encapsulates the essence of vibrancy and heritage, inviting enthusiasts to savor the enchanting fusion of tradition and innovation that defines the Scottish cocktail culture.

Ingredients:

- 1 ounce Scotch whisky
- 3/4 ounce sweet vermouth
- 3/4 ounce orange juice
- 1/2 ounce rosehip syrup
- Orange twist, for garnish
- Ice cubes

Instructions:

1. Fill a shaker with ice cubes.
2. Add the Scotch whisky, sweet vermouth, orange juice, and rosehip syrup to the shaker.
3. Shake the mixture vigorously for about 15 seconds to chill the ingredients.
4. Strain the mixture into a chilled cocktail glass.
5. Express the oils from an orange twist over the cocktail by squeezing it over the glass.
6. Garnish the Rosehip Blood and Sand with the orange twist for a citrusy and aromatic touch.
7. Serve and enjoy this invigorating and flavorful Scottish-inspired cocktail, celebrating the rich history and dynamic flavors that epitomize the spirit of Scottish conviviality and cocktail craftsmanship.

38. Rosehip Penicillin (Scotland)

The Rosehip Penicillin cocktail is a testament to the rich Scottish tradition of whisky craftsmanship and the enduring legacy of creating bold and innovative cocktails. Drawing inspiration from the classic Penicillin, celebrated for its robust and invigorating flavors, this unique adaptation infuses the traditional cocktail with the tangy sweetness of rosehip, creating a delightful libation that captures the spirit of Scottish innovation and the art of savoring complex and well-balanced libations. The Rosehip Penicillin encapsulates the essence of creativity and heritage, inviting enthusiasts to savor the enchanting fusion of tradition and innovation that defines the Scottish cocktail culture.

Ingredients:

- 2 ounces blended Scotch whisky
- 3/4 ounce fresh lemon juice
- 3/4 ounce honey syrup
- 1/4 ounce rosehip syrup
- 1/4 ounce smoky Scotch whisky
- Candied ginger, for garnish
- Ice cubes

Instructions:

1. In a shaker, combine the blended Scotch whisky, fresh lemon juice, honey syrup, and rosehip syrup.
2. Add ice cubes to the shaker and shake vigorously for about 15-20 seconds.
3. Strain the mixture into a rocks glass filled with a large ice cube.
4. Float the smoky Scotch whisky on top of the cocktail.
5. Garnish the Rosehip Penicillin with a piece of candied ginger for a sweet and spicy touch.
6. Serve and enjoy this invigorating and flavorful Scottish-inspired cocktail, celebrating the rich history and dynamic flavors that epitomize the spirit of Scottish innovation and cocktail craftsmanship.

39. Rosehip Drambuie Collins (Scotland)

The Rosehip Drambuie Collins is a celebration of the rich Scottish culinary heritage and the art of crafting refreshing and vibrant cocktails. Drawing inspiration from the classic Tom Collins, renowned for its invigorating and lively qualities, this unique adaptation infuses the traditional cocktail with the tangy sweetness of rosehip, creating a delightful libation that embodies the spirit of Scottish conviviality and the appreciation of well-balanced libations. The Rosehip Drambuie Collins encapsulates the essence of vibrancy and heritage, inviting enthusiasts to savor the enchanting fusion of tradition and innovation that defines the Scottish cocktail culture.

Ingredients:

- 2 ounces Drambuie
- 1 ounce fresh lemon juice
- 1/2 ounce rosehip syrup
- Club soda
- Lemon wheel, for garnish
- Rosemary sprig, for garnish
- Ice cubes

Instructions:

1. Fill a Collins glass with ice cubes.
2. Pour the Drambuie, fresh lemon juice, and rosehip syrup into the glass.
3. Stir the mixture gently to combine the ingredients.
4. Top off the glass with club soda.
5. Garnish the Rosehip Drambuie Collins with a lemon wheel and a rosemary sprig for a fresh and aromatic touch.
6. Serve and enjoy this invigorating and flavorful Scottish-inspired cocktail, celebrating the rich history and dynamic flavors that epitomize the spirit of Scottish conviviality and cocktail craftsmanship.

40. Rosehip Highland Fling (Scotland)

Drawing inspiration from the lively Highland Fling dance, celebrated for its energy and exuberance, this unique cocktail infuses the traditional libation with the tangy sweetness of rosehip, creating a delightful concoction that captures the spirit of Scottish merriment and the art of savoring vibrant and dynamic libations. The Rosehip Highland Fling encapsulates the essence of liveliness and heritage, inviting enthusiasts to relish the enchanting fusion of tradition and innovation that defines the Scottish cocktail culture.

Ingredients:

- 1 1/2 ounces Scotch whisky
- 3/4 ounce rosehip syrup
- 1/2 ounce fresh lemon juice
- 2 ounces apple cider
- Dash of bitters
- Apple slice, for garnish
- Cinnamon stick, for garnish
- Ice cubes

Instructions:

1. In a shaker, combine the Scotch whisky, rosehip syrup, fresh lemon juice, apple cider, and a dash of bitters.
2. Add ice cubes to the shaker and shake vigorously for about 15 seconds.
3. Strain the mixture into a rocks glass filled with fresh ice.
4. Garnish the Rosehip Highland Fling with an apple slice and a cinnamon stick for a fragrant and flavorful touch.
5. Serve and enjoy this invigorating and flavorful Scottish-inspired cocktail, celebrating the rich history and lively flavors that epitomize the spirit of Scottish revelry and cocktail craftsmanship.

41. Rosehip Moscow Mule (Russia)

The Rosehip Moscow Mule is a fusion of the rich Russian culinary heritage and the art of crafting refreshing and zesty cocktails. Drawing inspiration from the classic Moscow Mule, celebrated for its crisp and invigorating flavors, this unique adaptation infuses the traditional cocktail with the tangy sweetness of rosehip, creating a delightful libation that captures the spirit of Russian conviviality and the appreciation of well-balanced libations. The Rosehip Moscow Mule encapsulates the essence of vibrancy and heritage, inviting enthusiasts to savor the enchanting fusion of tradition and innovation that defines the Russian cocktail culture.

Ingredients:

- 2 ounces vodka
- 1/2 ounce rosehip syrup
- 1/2 ounce fresh lime juice
- 4 ounces ginger beer
- Lime wedge, for garnish
- Rosemary sprig, for garnish
- Ice cubes

Instructions:

1. Fill a copper mug with ice cubes.
2. Pour the vodka and rosehip syrup over the ice.
3. Add the fresh lime juice to the mug and stir gently to combine the ingredients.
4. Top off the mug with ginger beer.
5. Garnish the Rosehip Moscow Mule with a lime wedge and a rosemary sprig for a fresh and aromatic touch.
6. Serve and enjoy this invigorating and flavorful Russian-inspired cocktail, celebrating the rich history and dynamic flavors that epitomize the spirit of Russian conviviality and cocktail craftsmanship.

42. Rosehip White Russian (Russia)

The Rosehip White Russian is a tribute to the rich Russian tradition of vodka craftsmanship and the enduring legacy of creating indulgent and creamy cocktails. Drawing inspiration from the classic White Russian, celebrated for its smooth and velvety flavors, this unique adaptation infuses the traditional cocktail with the tangy sweetness of rosehip, creating a delightful libation that captures the spirit of Russian indulgence and the appreciation of well-balanced libations. The Rosehip White Russian encapsulates the essence of luxury and heritage, inviting enthusiasts to relish the enchanting fusion of tradition and innovation that defines the Russian cocktail culture.

Ingredients:

- 1 1/2 ounces vodka
- 1/2 ounce coffee liqueur
- 1/2 ounce rosehip syrup
- 1 ounce heavy cream
- Ice cubes

Instructions:

1. Fill an old-fashioned glass with ice cubes.
2. Pour the vodka and coffee liqueur over the ice.
3. Add the rosehip syrup to the glass and stir gently to combine the ingredients.
4. Float the heavy cream on top of the cocktail.
5. Serve and enjoy this indulgent and flavorful Russian-inspired cocktail, celebrating the rich history and luxurious flavors that epitomize the spirit of Russian indulgence and cocktail craftsmanship.

43. Rosehip Black Russian (Russia)

Drawing inspiration from the classic Black Russian, renowned for its rich and decadent flavors, this unique adaptation infuses the traditional cocktail with the tangy sweetness of rosehip, creating a delightful libation that captures the spirit of Russian sophistication and the art of savoring robust and well-balanced libations. The Rosehip Black Russian encapsulates the essence of depth and heritage, inviting enthusiasts to relish the enchanting fusion of tradition and innovation that defines the Russian cocktail culture.

Ingredients:

- 1 1/2 ounces vodka
- 3/4 ounce coffee liqueur
- 1/4 ounce rosehip syrup
- Coffee beans, for garnish
- Ice cubes

Instructions:

1. Fill an old-fashioned glass with ice cubes.
2. Pour the vodka and coffee liqueur over the ice.
3. Drizzle the rosehip syrup over the cocktail.
4. Stir gently to combine the ingredients.
5. Garnish the Rosehip Black Russian with a few coffee beans for a rich and aromatic touch.
6. Serve and enjoy this indulgent and flavorful Russian-inspired cocktail, celebrating the rich history and luxurious flavors that epitomize the spirit of Russian sophistication and cocktail craftsmanship.

44. Rosehip Basil Martini (Russia)

The Rosehip Basil Martini pays tribute to the aromatic herb gardens of Russia and the harmonious balance of herbal and tangy notes in this sophisticated cocktail. Drawing from the classic Vodka Martini, this adaptation infuses the traditional recipe with the herbaceous essence of basil, creating a delightful libation that captures the essence of Russian sophistication and the appreciation of well-balanced cocktails.

Ingredients:

2 1/2 ounces vodka
1/2 ounce dry vermouth
1/4 ounce rosehip syrup
2-3 fresh basil leaves
Lemon twist, for garnish
Ice cubes

Instructions:

1. Fill a mixing glass with ice cubes.
2. Pour the vodka, dry vermouth, and rosehip syrup over the ice.
3. Stir the mixture vigorously for about 30 seconds to chill the ingredients.
4. Strain the mixture into a chilled martini glass.
5. Express the oils from a lemon twist over the cocktail by squeezing it over the glass.
6. Garnish the Rosehip Vodka Martini with crushed and twisted basil for a savory and aromatic touch.
7. Serve and enjoy this sophisticated and flavorful Russian-inspired cocktail, celebrating the rich history and refined flavors that epitomize the spirit of Russian refinement and cocktail craftsmanship.

45. Rosehip Bloody Ceaser (Canada)

The Rosehip Bloody Caesar pays homage to the rich Canadian tradition of the iconic Caesar cocktail, celebrated for its bold and savory flavors. Drawing inspiration from this classic Canadian libation, the Rosehip Bloody Caesar infuses the traditional recipe with the tangy sweetness of rosehip and the savory addition of chopped clams, creating a unique and delightful drink that encapsulates the essence of Canadian culinary innovation and the appreciation of well-balanced libations.

Ingredients:
- 1 1/2 ounces vodka
- 3 ounces tomato juice
- 1/2 ounce freshly squeezed lemon juice
- 1/4 ounce rosehip syrup
- 1/4 teaspoon freshly grated horseradish
- 2 dashes Worcestershire sauce
- 2 dashes hot sauce
- Pinch of celery salt
- Pinch of freshly ground black pepper
- Chopped clams
- Celery stalk, for garnish
- Lime wedge, for garnish
- Ice cubes

Instructions:
1. Rim a highball glass with celery salt and fill it with ice cubes.
2. In a shaker, combine the vodka, tomato juice, freshly squeezed lemon juice, rosehip syrup, freshly grated horseradish, Worcestershire sauce, hot sauce, celery salt, and black pepper.
3. Shake the mixture vigorously for about 15-20 seconds.
4. Strain the mixture into the prepared highball glass.
5. Add the chopped clams to the cocktail for a unique and savory twist.
6. Garnish the Rosehip Bloody Caesar with a celery stalk and a lime wedge for a refreshing and aromatic touch.
7. Serve and enjoy this bold and flavorful Canadian-inspired cocktail, celebrating the rich history and dynamic flavors that epitomize the spirit of Canadian culinary innovation and cocktail craftsmanship.

46. Rosehip Mimosa (France)

The Rosehip Mimosa is a celebration of the elegant French culinary tradition and the art of crafting light and effervescent cocktails. Drawing inspiration from the classic Mimosa, renowned for its sparkling and citrusy flavors, this unique adaptation infuses the traditional cocktail with the tangy sweetness of rosehip, creating a delightful libation that captures the spirit of French sophistication and the appreciation of well-balanced libations.

The Rosehip Mimosa encapsulates the essence of vibrancy and heritage, inviting enthusiasts to savor the enchanting fusion of tradition and innovation that defines the French cocktail culture.

Ingredients:

- 2 ounces chilled Champagne or sparkling wine
- 1 ounce freshly squeezed orange juice
- 1/2 ounce rosehip syrup
- Orange twist, for garnish

Instructions:

1. In a Champagne flute, combine the chilled Champagne or sparkling wine and freshly squeezed orange juice.
2. Add the rosehip syrup to the flute and stir gently to combine the ingredients.
3. Garnish the Rosehip Mimosa with an orange twist for a citrusy and aromatic touch.
4. Serve and enjoy this invigorating and flavorful French-inspired cocktail, celebrating the rich history and dynamic flavors that epitomize the spirit of French conviviality and cocktail craftsmanship.

47. Rosehip Kir Royale (France)

The Rosehip Kir Royale is a tribute to the rich French tradition of elegance and the enduring legacy of crafting sophisticated and vibrant cocktails. Drawing inspiration from the classic Kir Royale, celebrated for its sparkling and balanced flavors, this unique adaptation infuses the traditional cocktail with the tangy sweetness of rosehip, creating a delightful libation that captures the spirit of French refinement and the appreciation of well-balanced libations. The Rosehip Kir Royale encapsulates the essence of sophistication and heritage, inviting enthusiasts to relish the enchanting fusion of tradition and innovation that defines the French cocktail culture.

Ingredients:

- 1/2 ounce rosehip syrup
- Chilled Champagne or sparkling wine
- Fresh raspberries, for garnish

Instructions:

1. Add the rosehip syrup to the bottom of a Champagne flute.
2. Top up the flute with chilled Champagne or sparkling wine.
3. Garnish the Rosehip Kir Royale with a few fresh raspberries for a vibrant and fruity touch.
4. Serve and enjoy this sophisticated and flavorful French-inspired cocktail, celebrating the rich history and refined flavors that epitomize the spirit of French elegance and cocktail craftsmanship.

48. Rosehip French 75 (France)

The Rosehip French 75 is a celebration of the classic French cocktail culture and the art of crafting sophisticated and effervescent drinks. Drawing inspiration from the iconic French 75, renowned for its refreshing and citrusy flavors, this unique adaptation infuses the traditional cocktail with the tangy sweetness of rosehip, creating a delightful libation that captures the essence of French sophistication and the appreciation of well-balanced libations.

The Rosehip French 75 encapsulates the spirit of celebration and heritage, inviting enthusiasts to savor the enchanting fusion of tradition and innovation that defines the French cocktail culture.

Ingredients:

- 1 1/2 ounces gin
- 1/2 ounce rosehip syrup
- 1/2 ounce freshly squeezed lemon juice
- Chilled Champagne or sparkling wine
- Lemon twist, for garnish

Instructions:

1. In a shaker, combine the gin, rosehip syrup, and freshly squeezed lemon juice.
2. Add ice to the shaker and shake vigorously for about 15-20 seconds.
3. Strain the mixture into a Champagne flute.
4. Top up the flute with chilled Champagne or sparkling wine.
5. Garnish the Rosehip French 75 with a lemon twist for a citrusy and aromatic touch.
6. Serve and enjoy this sophisticated and flavorful French-inspired cocktail, celebrating the rich history and dynamic flavors that epitomize the spirit of French elegance and cocktail craftsmanship.

49. Rosehip Sidecar (France)

The Rosehip Sidecar is a tribute to the rich French tradition of elegant mixology and the enduring legacy of crafting refined and balanced cocktails. Drawing inspiration from the classic Sidecar, celebrated for its sophisticated and citrusy flavors, this unique adaptation infuses the traditional cocktail with the tangy sweetness of rosehip, creating a delightful libation that captures the spirit of French refinement and the appreciation of well-balanced libations. The Rosehip Sidecar encapsulates the essence of sophistication and heritage, inviting enthusiasts to relish the enchanting fusion of tradition and innovation that defines the French cocktail culture.

Ingredients:

- 2 ounces Cognac
- 1/2 ounce triple sec
- 1/2 ounce rosehip syrup
- 3/4 ounce freshly squeezed lemon juice
- Lemon twist, for garnish
- Ice cubes

Instructions:

1. Rim a chilled cocktail glass with sugar and set it aside.
2. In a shaker, combine the Cognac, triple sec, rosehip syrup, and freshly squeezed lemon juice.
3. Add ice to the shaker and shake vigorously for about 15-20 seconds.
4. Strain the mixture into the prepared cocktail glass.
5. Garnish the Rosehip Sidecar with a lemon twist for a citrusy and aromatic touch.
6. Serve and enjoy this sophisticated and flavorful French-inspired cocktail, celebrating the rich history and nuanced flavors that epitomize the spirit of French refinement and cocktail craftsmanship.

50. Rosehip Champagne Cocktail (France)

The Rosehip Champagne Cocktail is a tribute to the French tradition of elegance and celebration, capturing the essence of joie de vivre and the art of crafting exquisite and effervescent libations. Drawing inspiration from the classic Champagne Cocktail, renowned for its timeless and sparkling flavors, this unique adaptation infuses the traditional drink with the tangy sweetness of rosehip, creating a delightful concoction that embodies the spirit of French sophistication and the appreciation of well-balanced libations.

The Rosehip Champagne Cocktail encapsulates the essence of festivity and heritage, inviting enthusiasts to relish the enchanting fusion of tradition and innovation that defines the French cocktail culture.

Ingredients:

- 1 sugar cube
- Angostura bitters
- 1/4 ounce rosehip syrup
- Chilled Champagne or sparkling wine
- Lemon twist, for garnish

Instructions:

1. Place a sugar cube in a Champagne flute and saturate it with a few dashes of Angostura bitters.
2. Add the rosehip syrup to the flute.
3. Top up the flute with chilled Champagne or sparkling wine.
4. Garnish the Rosehip Champagne Cocktail with a lemon twist for a citrusy and aromatic touch.
5. Serve and enjoy this sparkling and flavorful French-inspired cocktail, celebrating the rich history and effervescent flavors that epitomize the spirit of French joie de vivre and cocktail craftsmanship.

Twenty Exotic Non-Alcoholic Rosehip Drinks

In the realm of vibrant and diverse beverage culture, the allure of rosehip-infused concoctions stands out as a testament to the art of crafting exotic and refreshing libations. With a rich history rooted in various culinary traditions across the globe, rosehip has found its way into an array of alcohol-free beverages, each bearing the distinct flavors and essence of their cultural origins. From the aromatic chai blends of India to the invigorating Thai tea variations, and the delicate Japanese tea latte innovations to the tantalizing concoctions of Korea, each sip of these rosehip-infused creations offers a journey through the nuanced flavors and cultural tapestries that define these unique global beverages. Join us as we delve into the world of the twenty most tantalizing and alcohol-free rosehip beverages, exploring their cultural significance and the delightful fusion of flavors that makes each of them a true testament to the art of beverage craftsmanship.

1. Rosehip Chai Tea (India)

Originating in the diverse and rich tapestry of Indian culinary traditions, the Rosehip Chai Tea is a testament to the country's love affair with aromatic spices and flavorful beverages. Infusing the soothing qualities of traditional chai with the tangy sweetness of rosehip, this delightful blend embodies the warmth and vibrancy of Indian culture, inviting enthusiasts to embark on a sensory journey through its nuanced flavors and aromatic charm.

Ingredients:

- 2 cups water
- 1 cinnamon stick
- 4-5 whole cloves
- 4-5 cardamom pods, lightly crushed
- 1-inch piece fresh ginger, sliced
- 2-3 black peppercorns
- 1 teaspoon loose black tea or 1 black tea bag
- 1 tablespoon rosehip syrup
- 1/2 cup milk (adjust according to preference)
- Sweetener (such as honey or sugar), to taste

Instructions:

1. In a saucepan, bring the water to a boil.
2. Add the cinnamon stick, cloves, cardamom pods, fresh ginger, and black peppercorns to the boiling water.
3. Reduce the heat and let the spices simmer for 5-7 minutes.
4. Add the black tea to the saucepan and let it steep for 2-3 minutes.
5. Stir in the rosehip syrup and milk, and simmer the mixture for an additional 2-3 minutes.
6. Strain the chai into cups or mugs.
7. Add sweetener as desired, and stir to combine.
8. Serve and enjoy the aromatic and invigorating Rosehip Chai Tea, savoring the rich flavors and cultural heritage it embodies.

2. Rosehip Lassi (India)

The Rosehip Lassi, originating from the diverse and vibrant culinary traditions of India, is a delightful and refreshing yogurt-based beverage infused with the tangy sweetness of rosehip. Known for its creamy texture and indulgent flavors, this lassi embodies the rich cultural heritage of India, offering a rejuvenating and exotic experience for the senses. Blending the wholesome goodness of yogurt with the invigorating essence of rosehip, this beverage is a celebration of India's love for rich, creamy concoctions that perfectly balance sweetness and tanginess.

Ingredients:

- 1 cup plain yogurt
- 1/2 cup milk
- 2 tablespoons rosehip syrup
- 1 tablespoon honey or sugar (adjust according to preference)
- 1/2 teaspoon ground cardamom
- Ice cubes
- Rose petals, for garnish (optional)

Instructions:

1. In a blender, combine the plain yogurt, milk, rosehip syrup, honey or sugar, and ground cardamom.
2. Blend the mixture until smooth and creamy.
3. Add a few ice cubes and blend again until the lassi reaches a smooth and frothy consistency.
4. Pour the Rosehip Lassi into glasses.
5. Garnish with rose petals for an extra touch of elegance (optional).
6. Serve chilled and enjoy the refreshing and creamy Rosehip Lassi, savoring the harmonious blend of flavors and the cultural richness it represents.

3. Rosehip Masala Chai (India)

Rosehip Masala Chai is a flavorful and aromatic beverage that fuses the rich Indian tradition of masala chai with the tangy sweetness of rosehip. This delightful concoction represents the harmonious blend of warming spices and the invigorating essence of rosehip, capturing the essence of India's love for bold and fragrant flavors. With its comforting aroma and rich depth of taste, Rosehip Masala Chai offers a sensory journey through the vibrant cultural tapestry of India, inviting enthusiasts to indulge in a cup of warmth and rejuvenation.

Ingredients:

- 2 cups water
- 1 cup milk
- 2-3 tablespoons loose black tea or 2 black tea bags
- 1 cinnamon stick
- 4-5 whole cloves
- 4-5 cardamom pods, lightly crushed
- 1-inch piece fresh ginger, sliced
- 2-3 black peppercorns
- 1 tablespoon rosehip syrup
- Sweetener (such as sugar or honey), to taste

Instructions:

1. In a saucepan, bring water to a boil.
2. Add the cinnamon stick, cloves, cardamom pods, fresh ginger, and black peppercorns to the boiling water.
3. Reduce the heat and let the spices simmer for 5-7 minutes.
4. Add the black tea to the saucepan and let it steep for 2-3 minutes.
5. Stir in the rosehip syrup and milk, and simmer the mixture for an additional 2-3 minutes.
6. Strain the chai into cups or mugs.
7. Add sweetener as desired, and stir to combine.
8. Serve and enjoy the aromatic and invigorating Rosehip Masala Chai, savoring the rich flavors and cultural heritage it embodies.

4. Rosehip Mango Lassi (India)

Rosehip Mango Lassi is a delightful and refreshing yogurt-based beverage that beautifully combines the tropical sweetness of mango with the tangy twist of rosehip, capturing the essence of India's love for rich and creamy concoctions. This lassi represents a harmonious fusion of flavors, offering a rejuvenating and exotic experience for the senses. With its smooth texture and vibrant taste, Rosehip Mango Lassi embodies the vibrancy and richness of Indian culinary traditions, inviting enthusiasts to indulge in a truly tropical and invigorating delight.

Ingredients:

- 1 cup plain yogurt
- 1 ripe mango, peeled and diced
- 2 tablespoons rosehip syrup
- 1 tablespoon honey or sugar (adjust according to preference)
- A pinch of ground cardamom
- Ice cubes
- Mango slices, for garnish (optional)

Instructions:

1. In a blender, combine the plain yogurt, diced mango, rosehip syrup, honey or sugar, and ground cardamom.
2. Blend the mixture until smooth and creamy.
3. Add a few ice cubes and blend again until the lassi reaches a smooth and frothy consistency.
4. Pour the Rosehip Mango Lassi into glasses.
5. Garnish with mango slices for an extra touch of tropical flair (optional).
6. Serve chilled and enjoy the refreshing and creamy Rosehip Mango Lassi, savoring the luscious blend of flavors and the cultural richness it represents.

5. Rosehip Spiced Tea (India)

Rosehip Spiced Tea, inspired by the rich and aromatic Indian tea tradition, is a delightful infusion that marries the tangy sweetness of rosehip with a medley of warm and fragrant spices. This aromatic blend exemplifies the essence of India's affinity for bold flavors and soothing beverages. With its comforting aroma and invigorating taste, Rosehip Spiced Tea provides a sensory experience that reflects the cultural tapestry and culinary heritage of India, inviting enthusiasts to relish a cup of warmth and exotic flavors.

Ingredients:

- 2 cups water
- 1 tablespoon loose black tea or 2 black tea bags
- 1 cinnamon stick
- 4-5 whole cloves
- 4-5 cardamom pods, lightly crushed
- 1-inch piece fresh ginger, sliced
- 2-3 black peppercorns
- 1 tablespoon rosehip syrup
- Sweetener (such as sugar or honey), to taste

Instructions:

1. In a saucepan, bring the water to a boil.
2. Add the cinnamon stick, cloves, cardamom pods, fresh ginger, and black peppercorns to the boiling water.
3. Reduce the heat and let the spices simmer for 5-7 minutes.
4. Add the black tea to the saucepan and let it steep for 2-3 minutes.
5. Stir in the rosehip syrup and sweetener, and simmer the mixture for an additional 2-3 minutes.
6. Strain the spiced tea into cups or mugs.
7. Serve and relish the fragrant and comforting Rosehip Spiced Tea, enjoying the blend of flavors that pay homage to the rich cultural heritage and love for aromatic teas in India.

6. Rosehip Thai Iced Tea (Thailand)

Rosehip Thai Iced Tea is a refreshing and aromatic beverage that combines the unique flavors of rosehip with the classic Thai iced tea, creating a delightful fusion of floral and spiced notes. This exotic concoction pays homage to Thailand's vibrant culinary heritage, offering a sweet and invigorating experience that captures the essence of the country's love for rich and flavorful drinks. With its creamy texture and captivating aroma, Rosehip Thai Iced Tea provides a sensory journey through the enchanting flavors of Thailand, inviting enthusiasts to indulge in a glass of cool and revitalizing indulgence.

Ingredients:

- 2 cups water
- 2 Thai tea bags
- 1 tablespoon rosehip syrup
- 2 tablespoons sweetened condensed milk
- Ice cubes
- Optional: half-and-half or evaporated milk for a creamier texture

Instructions:

1. Boil the water in a saucepan and add the Thai tea bags. Let the tea steep for 5-7 minutes.
2. Remove the tea bags and stir in the rosehip syrup.
3. Allow the tea to cool to room temperature, then refrigerate until chilled.
4. Fill glasses with ice cubes and pour the chilled tea over the ice.
5. Drizzle sweetened condensed milk over the tea, allowing it to sink to the bottom.
6. Optionally, add a splash of half-and-half or evaporated milk for a creamier texture.
7. Stir gently before serving to mix in the milk.
8. Enjoy the invigorating and creamy Rosehip Thai Iced Tea, savoring the delightful blend of flavors that reflect the exotic charm of Thailand.

7. Rosehip Thai Iced Coffee (Thailand)

Rosehip Thai Iced Coffee is a tantalizing blend that fuses the rich flavors of coffee with the subtle tang of rosehip, creating a refreshing and aromatic beverage that captures the essence of Thailand's vibrant culinary culture. This invigorating concoction pays homage to the country's love for bold and dynamic flavors, offering a delightful balance between the robustness of coffee and the floral notes of rosehip. With its creamy texture and captivating aroma, Rosehip Thai Iced Coffee provides a sensory journey through the enchanting and exotic flavors of Thailand, inviting enthusiasts to indulge in a glass of cool and revitalizing indulgence.

Ingredients:

- 2 cups strongly brewed coffee, chilled
- 1 tablespoon rosehip syrup
- 2 tablespoons sweetened condensed milk
- Ice cubes
- Optional: half-and-half or evaporated milk for a creamier texture

Instructions:

1. Brew a strong pot of coffee and let it cool to room temperature. Refrigerate until chilled.
2. In a glass, combine the chilled coffee with the rosehip syrup.
3. Fill another glass with ice cubes and pour the coffee mixture over the ice.
4. Drizzle sweetened condensed milk over the coffee, allowing it to sink to the bottom.
5. Optionally, add a splash of half-and-half or evaporated milk for a creamier texture.
6. Stir gently before serving to mix in the milk.
7. Enjoy the invigorating and creamy Rosehip Thai Iced Coffee, savoring the harmonious blend of flavors that reflect the exotic charm and culinary vibrancy of Thailand.

8. Rosehip Thai Tea Smoothie (Thailand)

Rosehip Thai Tea Smoothie is a delectable fusion of the iconic Thai tea's robust flavors and the tangy sweetness of rosehip, creating a luscious and invigorating beverage that embodies the essence of Thailand's rich culinary heritage. This refreshing smoothie pays homage to the country's love for vibrant and exotic flavors, offering a delightful balance between the creamy texture of the smoothie and the aromatic notes of rosehip and Thai tea.

With its velvety consistency and captivating aroma, Rosehip Thai Tea Smoothie provides a sensory journey through the enchanting and tropical flavors of Thailand, inviting enthusiasts to indulge in a glass of cool and revitalizing indulgence.

Ingredients:

- 1 cup strongly brewed Thai tea, chilled
- 1 tablespoon rosehip syrup
- 1 ripe banana, peeled and sliced
- 1/2 cup plain or vanilla yogurt
- 1/2 cup milk of choice
- 1 tablespoon honey or sugar (adjust to taste)
- Ice cubes
- Optional: whipped cream and a sprinkle of cinnamon for garnish

Instructions:

1. In a blender, combine the chilled Thai tea, rosehip syrup, sliced banana, yogurt, milk, and honey or sugar.
2. Add a handful of ice cubes to the blender for a frosty texture.
3. Blend the mixture on high speed until smooth and creamy.
4. Pour the smoothie into glasses.
5. Optionally, top with whipped cream and a sprinkle of cinnamon for an extra touch of indulgence.
6. Serve chilled and enjoy the tropical and creamy Rosehip Thai Tea Smoothie, savoring the harmonious blend of flavors that reflect the exotic charm and culinary vibrancy of Thailand.

9. Rosehip Thai Tea Lemonade (Thailand)

Rosehip Thai Tea Lemonade is a revitalizing and citrusy beverage that combines the unique flavors of Thai tea and the tangy twist of rosehip with a surprising touch of lemongrass, creating a refreshing and aromatic concoction that embodies the essence of Thailand's vibrant culinary culture.

This invigorating lemonade pays homage to the country's love for bold and dynamic flavors, offering a delightful balance between the robustness of Thai tea, the floral notes of rosehip, and the zesty essence of lemongrass. With its bright and lively flavors, Rosehip Thai Tea Lemonade provides a sensory journey through the enchanting and exotic flavors of Thailand, inviting enthusiasts to indulge in a glass of cool and revitalizing indulgence.

Ingredients:

- 2 cups strongly brewed Thai tea, chilled
- 1/2 cup rosehip syrup
- 1/2 cup freshly squeezed lemon juice
- 4 cups cold water
- 1/4 cup lemongrass simple syrup
- Ice cubes
- Lemon slices and lemongrass stalks for garnish

Instructions:

1. In a pitcher, combine the chilled Thai tea, rosehip syrup, freshly squeezed lemon juice, and cold water.
2. Stir well to combine all the ingredients.
3. Add the lemongrass simple syrup and mix thoroughly.
4. Fill glasses with ice cubes and pour the lemonade over the ice.
5. Garnish with lemon slices and lemongrass stalks for an extra touch of tropical flair.
6. Stir gently before serving to ensure all the flavors are well incorporated.
7. Enjoy the invigorating and citrusy Rosehip Thai Tea Lemonade, savoring the harmonious blend of flavors that reflect the exotic charm and culinary vibrancy of Thailand.

10. Rosehip Thai Tea Soda (Thailand)

Rosehip Thai Tea Soda is a delightful and effervescent beverage that harmoniously blends the rich and robust flavors of Thai tea with the tangy sweetness of rosehip, creating a refreshing and bubbly drink that encapsulates the essence of Thailand's vibrant culinary scene.

This invigorating soda pays homage to the country's love for bold and dynamic flavors, offering a delightful balance between the complexity of Thai tea and the floral notes of rosehip. With its fizzy texture and captivating aroma, Rosehip Thai Tea Soda provides a sensory journey through the enchanting and exotic flavors of Thailand, inviting enthusiasts to indulge in a glass of cool and revitalizing effervescence.

Ingredients:

- 1 cup strongly brewed Thai tea, chilled
- 2 tablespoons rosehip syrup
- 1 can of soda water or club soda, chilled
- Ice cubes
- Fresh mint leaves or basil leaves for garnish

Instructions:

1. In a glass, combine the chilled Thai tea and rosehip syrup.
2. Fill the glass with ice cubes.
3. Slowly pour the chilled soda water or club soda into the glass.
4. Gently stir the mixture to combine the flavors.
5. Garnish with fresh mint leaves or basil leaves for an added touch of freshness.
6. Serve immediately and enjoy the refreshing and bubbly Rosehip Thai Tea Soda, savoring the delightful blend of flavors that reflect the exotic charm and culinary vibrancy of Thailand.

11. Rosehip Matcha Latte (Japan)

Rosehip Matcha Latte is a harmonious fusion of the vibrant Japanese matcha tea and the tangy sweetness of rosehip, creating a smooth and invigorating beverage that captures the essence of Japan's centuries-old tea culture. This modern twist on a traditional favorite pays homage to Japan's profound appreciation for natural flavors and meticulous preparation methods. With its rich and creamy texture and captivating aroma, Rosehip Matcha Latte offers a sensory experience that reflects the cultural richness and culinary finesse of Japan, inviting enthusiasts to savor a cup of warm and revitalizing indulgence.

History of Matcha:

Matcha holds a significant place in Japanese tea ceremonies, tracing its roots back to the 12th century when it was introduced to Japan by Buddhist monks. It became an integral part of Zen meditation practices, celebrated for its ability to enhance focus and mindfulness. Made from finely ground green tea leaves, matcha is renowned for its vibrant green color and its numerous health benefits, including a high concentration of antioxidants and amino acids. The intricate process of growing, harvesting, and stone-grinding the tea leaves contributes to matcha's unique flavor profile and velvety texture. With its cultural significance and esteemed reputation, matcha continues to be cherished in Japan and around the world for its exquisite taste and holistic properties.

Ingredients:

- 1 teaspoon matcha powder
- 2 tablespoons hot water
- 1 tablespoon rosehip syrup
- 1 cup milk of choice
- Sweetener (such as honey or sugar), to taste

Instructions:

1. In a bowl, whisk matcha powder with hot water until frothy and well combined.
2. Stir in the rosehip syrup.
3. In a saucepan, heat the milk until steaming (not boiling).
4. Pour the steamed milk into the matcha mixture and stir gently.
5. Add sweetener to taste, if desired.
6. Pour the Rosehip Matcha Latte into a cup.
7. Serve and relish the velvety and invigorating Rosehip Matcha Latte, savoring the enchanting blend of flavors that reflect the rich cultural heritage of Japan.

12. Rosehip Hojicha Latte (Japan)

Rosehip Hojicha Latte is a comforting and earthy beverage that marries the roasted tones of Hojicha tea with the tangy sweetness of rosehip, offering a soothing and invigorating experience that pays homage to Japan's cherished tea culture. This unique combination of flavors highlights the country's appreciation for nuanced tastes and meticulous preparation methods. With its warm and inviting aroma, Rosehip Hojicha Latte provides a sensory journey through the cultural richness and culinary finesse of Japan, inviting enthusiasts to indulge in a cup of rich and revitalizing indulgence.

History of Hojicha:

Hojicha is a roasted green tea that holds a special place in Japanese tea traditions. Its origins can be traced back to the 1920s in Kyoto, Japan, where it was first crafted as a way to repurpose leftover tea leaves. Through the roasting process, the tea leaves develop a distinctive reddish-brown hue and a rich, toasty flavor profile, setting it apart from other Japanese green teas. Hojicha is celebrated for its gentle, low caffeine content and its warm, nutty undertones that offer a comforting and mellow drinking experience. With its humble beginnings and growing popularity, Hojicha has become a beloved staple in Japanese tea culture, cherished for its soothing properties and distinctive taste.

Ingredients:

- 1 tablespoon Hojicha tea leaves or 1 Hojicha tea bag
- 1 cup hot water
- 1 tablespoon rosehip syrup
- 1 cup milk of choice
- Sweetener (such as honey or sugar), to taste

Instructions:

1. Steep the Hojicha tea leaves or tea bag in hot water for 3-5 minutes.
2. Strain the tea into a saucepan and discard the tea leaves or bag.
3. Stir in the rosehip syrup.
4. In the same saucepan, heat the milk until steaming (not boiling).
5. Pour the steamed milk into the Hojicha and rosehip mixture and stir gently.
6. Add sweetener to taste, if desired.
7. Pour the Rosehip Hojicha Latte into a cup.
8. Serve and enjoy the comforting and aromatic Rosehip Hojicha Latte, savoring the rich blend of flavors that reflect the cultural heritage and love for tea in Japan.

13. Rosehip Genmaicha Latte (Japan)

Rosehip Genmaicha Latte is a delightful and comforting beverage that seamlessly blends the nutty flavors of Genmaicha tea with the tangy sweetness of rosehip, offering a rich and invigorating experience that pays homage to Japan's profound tea culture. This unique fusion of flavors represents the country's commitment to craftsmanship and its appreciation for nuanced taste profiles. With its warm and toasty aroma, Rosehip Genmaicha Latte provides a sensory journey through the cultural richness and culinary finesse of Japan, inviting enthusiasts to savor a cup of soothing and revitalizing indulgence.

History of Genmaicha:

Genmaicha, also known as "popcorn tea," is a traditional Japanese green tea that dates back to the 15th century. It is characterized by the unique addition of toasted brown rice kernels, which lend the tea its distinctive nutty flavor and aroma. The origins of Genmaicha can be traced to the frugal practices of Japanese tea farmers who mixed leftover tea leaves with roasted rice as a way to extend their tea supply. Over time, this humble blend gained popularity for its comforting and balanced taste, becoming a beloved everyday beverage in Japan. With its rustic charm and warm, earthy notes, Genmaicha continues to be celebrated for its soothing properties and distinctive flavor, embodying the essence of Japanese tea culture.

Recipe:

Ingredients:

- 1 tablespoon Genmaicha tea leaves or 1 Genmaicha tea bag
- 1 cup hot water
- 1 tablespoon rosehip syrup
- 1 cup milk of choice
- Sweetener (such as honey or sugar), to taste

Instructions:

1. Steep the Genmaicha tea leaves or tea bag in hot water for 3-5 minutes.
2. Strain the tea into a saucepan and discard the tea leaves or bag.
3. Stir in the rosehip syrup.
4. In the same saucepan, heat the milk until steaming (not boiling).
5. Pour the steamed milk into the Genmaicha and rosehip mixture and stir gently.
6. Add sweetener to taste, if desired.
7. Pour the Rosehip Genmaicha Latte into a cup.
8. Serve and relish the comforting and aromatic Rosehip Genmaicha Latte, savoring the harmonious blend of flavors that reflect the cultural heritage and love for tea in Japan.

14. Rosehip Yuzu Tea (Japan)

Rosehip Yuzu Tea is a vibrant and citrusy beverage that combines the zesty flavors of yuzu with the tangy sweetness of rosehip, offering a rejuvenating and invigorating experience that pays homage to Japan's revered culinary traditions. This unique blend of flavors reflects the country's appreciation for fresh and aromatic ingredients, showcasing the versatility and distinctiveness of Japanese cuisine. With its bright and refreshing aroma, Rosehip Yuzu Tea provides a sensory journey through the cultural richness and culinary finesse of Japan, inviting enthusiasts to relish a cup of revitalizing and exotic indulgence.

History of Yuzu:

Yuzu is a prized citrus fruit that has been cultivated in East Asia for centuries, with its origins tracing back to China and Tibet. It made its way to Japan during the Tang Dynasty, around the 7th century, and has since become an integral part of Japanese cuisine and culture. Renowned for its fragrant aroma and distinctively tart flavor, yuzu is celebrated for its culinary versatility, as its juice, zest, and peel are used in a variety of dishes and beverages. From enhancing savory dishes to brightening desserts and beverages, yuzu has established itself as a beloved and iconic ingredient, embodying the essence of Japanese culinary heritage and its emphasis on fresh, natural flavors.

Ingredients:

- 2 cups water
- 1/2 cup yuzu juice
- 1 tablespoon dried rosehips
- 2 tablespoons honey or sweetener of choice
- Optional: a few slices of fresh yuzu for garnish

Instructions:

1. In a saucepan, combine the water, yuzu juice, and dried rosehips.
2. Bring the mixture to a gentle boil, then reduce the heat and let it simmer for 15-20 minutes.
3. Remove the saucepan from the heat and strain the tea into a teapot or a pitcher.
4. Stir in the honey or sweetener of choice, adjusting the sweetness to your preference.
5. Serve the Rosehip Yuzu Tea in cups or mugs.
6. Optionally, garnish each serving with a slice of fresh yuzu for an extra burst of citrusy flavor and aroma.
7. Enjoy the revitalizing and aromatic Rosehip Yuzu Tea, savoring the harmonious blend of flavors that reflect the cultural heritage and love for fresh ingredients in Japan.

15. Rosehip Sakura Tea (Japan)

Rosehip Sakura Tea is an exquisite and delicate beverage that combines the floral essence of cherry blossoms, known as sakura in Japan, with the tangy sweetness of rosehip, offering a fragrant and invigorating experience that pays homage to Japan's profound appreciation for natural beauty and delicate flavors. This unique blend captures the ephemeral charm of the cherry blossom season, showcasing the country's deep cultural reverence for these iconic blooms. With its gentle and enchanting aroma, Rosehip Sakura Tea provides a sensory journey through the ethereal and poetic essence of Japan, inviting enthusiasts to savor a cup of soothing and revitalizing indulgence.

Ingredients:

- 2 cups water
- 1 tablespoon dried sakura blossoms or sakura tea leaves
- 1 tablespoon dried rosehips
- 2 tablespoons honey or sweetener of choice
- Optional: a few fresh cherry blossoms for garnish

Instructions:

1. In a saucepan, bring the water to a gentle boil.
2. Add the dried sakura blossoms or sakura tea leaves and dried rosehips to the water.
3. Let the mixture simmer for 10-15 minutes to infuse the flavors.
4. Remove the saucepan from the heat and strain the tea into a teapot or a pitcher.
5. Stir in the honey or sweetener of choice, adjusting the sweetness to your preference.
6. Serve the Rosehip Sakura Tea in cups or mugs.
7. Optionally, garnish each serving with a few fresh cherry blossoms for an elegant touch and a delicate floral aroma.
8. Enjoy the soothing and aromatic Rosehip Sakura Tea, savoring the harmonious blend of flavors that reflect the cultural heritage and reverence for natural beauty in Japan.

16. Rosehip Calpis (Japan)

Rosehip Calpis is a delightful and refreshing beverage that marries the tangy flavors of rosehip with the creamy and slightly acidic taste of Calpis, offering a unique and invigorating experience that pays homage to Japan's cherished culinary culture. This fusion of flavors represents the country's dedication to innovative and harmonious taste combinations, showcasing the versatility and distinctiveness of Japanese beverages. With its creamy texture and bright, fruity aroma, Rosehip Calpis provides a sensory journey through the cultural richness and culinary finesse of Japan, inviting enthusiasts to indulge in a glass of cool and revitalizing indulgence.

Calpis, known as Calpico outside of Japan, is a popular Japanese uncarbonated soft drink that boasts a milky and slightly acidic flavor profile. It was first developed in 1919 by Kaiun Mishima, a Japanese dairy farmer, and its unique taste quickly gained popularity among consumers. Calpis is created through a fermentation process using lactic acid bacteria, giving it a distinct tangy flavor that is both refreshing and satisfying. It has since become a beloved beverage in Japan and is often used as a base for various flavored drinks and cocktails.

Ingredients:

- 1 cup Calpis or Calpico
- 2 tablespoons rosehip syrup
- Ice cubes
- Fresh mint leaves or lemon slices for garnish

Instructions:

1. In a glass, combine the Calpis or Calpico with the rosehip syrup.
2. Stir well to blend the flavors.
3. Add ice cubes to the glass to chill the beverage.
4. Garnish with fresh mint leaves or a slice of lemon for an added touch of freshness.
5. Serve the Rosehip Calpis immediately and enjoy the delightful and invigorating fusion of flavors that reflect the cultural heritage and love for innovative beverages in Japan.

17. Rosehip Ramune (Japan)

Rosehip Calpis is a delightful and refreshing beverage that marries the tangy flavors of rosehip with the creamy and slightly acidic taste of Calpis, offering a unique and invigorating experience that pays homage to Japan's cherished culinary culture. This fusion of flavors represents the country's dedication to innovative and harmonious taste combinations, showcasing the versatility and distinctiveness of Japanese beverages. With its creamy texture and bright, fruity aroma, Rosehip Calpis provides a sensory journey through the cultural richness and culinary finesse of Japan, inviting enthusiasts to indulge in a glass of cool and revitalizing indulgence.

Calpis, known as Calpico outside of Japan, is a popular Japanese uncarbonated soft drink that boasts a milky and slightly acidic flavor profile. It was first developed in 1919 by Kaiun Mishima, a Japanese dairy farmer, and its unique taste quickly gained popularity among consumers. Calpis is created through a fermentation process using lactic acid bacteria, giving it a distinct tangy flavor that is both refreshing and satisfying. It has since become a beloved beverage in Japan and is often used as a base for various flavored drinks and cocktails.

Ingredients:

- 1 cup Calpis or Calpico
- 2 tablespoons rosehip syrup
- Ice cubes
- Fresh mint leaves or lemon slices for garnish

Instructions:

1. In a glass, combine the Calpis or Calpico with the rosehip syrup.
2. Stir well to blend the flavors.
3. Add ice cubes to the glass to chill the beverage.
4. Garnish with fresh mint leaves or a slice of lemon for an added touch of freshness.
5. Serve the Rosehip Calpis immediately and enjoy the delightful and invigorating fusion of flavors that reflect the cultural heritage and love for innovative beverages in Japan.

18. Rosehip Melon Soda (Japan)

Rosehip Melon Soda is a delightful and refreshing beverage that combines the tangy sweetness of rosehip with the luscious flavors of homemade melon soda, offering a uniquely invigorating and fruity experience that pays homage to Japan's renowned culinary culture. This fusion of flavors showcases the country's dedication to creating innovative and enjoyable beverages, highlighting the freshness and vibrancy of Japanese ingredients. With its sparkling texture and bright, fruity aroma, Rosehip Melon Soda provides a delightful journey through the cultural richness and culinary finesse of Japan, inviting enthusiasts to relish a glass of cool and revitalizing indulgence.

To make homemade melon soda, you'll need fresh melon juice, soda water, and a touch of sweetness. Choose a ripe and fragrant melon, such as cantaloupe or honeydew, to extract the juice. Here's a simple recipe for preparing this delightful beverage:

Ingredients:

- 1 cup fresh melon juice
- 1 cup soda water
- 2 tablespoons rosehip syrup or fresh rosehip extract
- Ice cubes
- Fresh mint leaves or melon slices for garnish

Instructions:

1. In a pitcher, combine the fresh melon juice and soda water.
2. Add the rosehip syrup or fresh rosehip extract and stir gently to incorporate the flavors.
3. Drop in a few ice cubes to chill the soda.
4. Stir once more to ensure the ingredients are well mixed.
5. Pour the Rosehip Melon Soda into individual glasses.
6. Garnish each glass with fresh mint leaves or slices of melon for an extra touch of freshness and visual appeal.
7. Serve the homemade Rosehip Melon Soda immediately and enjoy the delightful and fruity fusion of flavors that reflect the cultural heritage and love for innovative beverages in Japan.

19. Rosehip Bubble Tea (Taiwan)

Rosehip Bubble Tea is a delightful and refreshing beverage that infuses the tangy notes of rosehip with the beloved and chewy tapioca pearls of traditional Taiwanese bubble tea, offering a uniquely invigorating and textured experience that pays homage to Taiwan's rich culinary heritage. This fusion of flavors highlights the country's dedication to creating innovative and enjoyable beverages, showcasing the versatility and playfulness of Taiwanese drink culture. With its vibrant texture and fruity aroma, Rosehip Bubble Tea provides a delightful journey through the cultural richness and culinary finesse of Taiwan, inviting enthusiasts to savor a glass of cool and revitalizing indulgence.

To prepare Rosehip Bubble Tea, you'll need rosehip tea, cooked tapioca pearls, and a sweetener of your choice. Here's a simple recipe to create this delightful beverage:

Ingredients:

- 1 cup brewed rosehip tea, cooled
- 1/2 cup cooked tapioca pearls
- 1/4 cup milk of your choice (optional)
- 2 tablespoons sweetener (such as simple syrup or honey)
- Ice cubes

Instructions:

1. In a tall glass, combine the brewed and cooled rosehip tea with the sweetener.
2. Add the cooked tapioca pearls to the glass.
3. If desired, pour in the milk of your choice to create a creamier texture.
4. Add ice cubes to chill the beverage.
5. Stir gently to combine all the ingredients.
6. Insert a wide straw and enjoy the delightful texture and fruity flavors of the Rosehip Bubble Tea, celebrating the playful and vibrant spirit of Taiwanese culinary culture.

20. Rosehip Wintermelon Tea (Taiwan)

Rosehip Wintermelon Tea is a refreshing and soothing beverage that blends the tangy essence of rosehip with the subtle and cooling flavor of wintermelon, offering a uniquely invigorating and revitalizing experience that pays homage to Taiwan's rich tea culture. This fusion of flavors highlights the country's dedication to creating innovative and enjoyable beverages, showcasing the versatility and depth of Taiwanese drink traditions. With its calming texture and delicate fruity aroma, Rosehip Wintermelon Tea provides a delightful journey through the cultural richness and culinary finesse of Taiwan, inviting enthusiasts to relish a cup of cool and rejuvenating indulgence.

To prepare Rosehip Wintermelon Tea, you'll need rosehip tea and wintermelon syrup. Here's a simple recipe to create this delightful beverage:

Ingredients:

- 1 cup brewed rosehip tea, cooled
- 1/2 cup wintermelon syrup
- Ice cubes
- Fresh mint leaves or slices of wintermelon for garnish

Instructions:

1. Making Wintermelon Syrup:

> To make the wintermelon syrup, you can chop fresh wintermelon into small pieces and blend it with an equal amount of sugar. Heat the mixture in a saucepan over low heat until the sugar dissolves and the mixture thickens into a syrup-like consistency. Strain the syrup to remove any pulp, and let it cool before use.

2. In a pitcher, combine the brewed and cooled rosehip tea with the wintermelon syrup.
3. Stir well to blend the flavors.
4. Add ice cubes to chill the beverage.
5. Pour the Rosehip Wintermelon Tea into individual glasses.
6. Garnish each glass with fresh mint leaves or slices of wintermelon for an added touch of freshness and visual appeal.
7. Serve the Rosehip Wintermelon Tea immediately and enjoy the delightful and soothing fusion of flavors that reflect the cultural heritage and love for refreshing beverages in Taiwan.

Substitution Tip: If wintermelon is not available, you can substitute it with other mild-flavored melons, such as honeydew or cantaloupe, to achieve a similar refreshing taste profile. Adjust the sweetness accordingly based on the natural sweetness of the melon used.

Rosehip Vinegars and Shrubs

In the realm of culinary exploration, the dynamic and versatile world of rosehips continues to captivate with its diverse applications. Among the many enchanting derivatives of this cherished fruit, rosehip vinegars and shrubs stand out as exceptional testaments to the art of preservation and infusion. Embodied in a harmonious blend of tangy sweetness and floral zest, these vinegars and shrubs have established their own niche in the culinary landscape, offering an enticing experience that transcends the ordinary.

In the context of this chapter, 'shrubs' refer to a type of beverage made by blending fruit-infused vinegar with sugar or honey, creating a sweet and tangy syrup that can be used to make refreshing drinks. The process of creating shrubs is revered as an ancient art, one that harnesses the essence of nature's bounty and transforms it into a delectable elixir. In this chapter, we embark on a journey that delves into the rich tapestry of rosehip vinegars and shrubs, exploring their origins, traditional significance, and contemporary resurgence in the global gastronomic scene.

From the verdant meadows of Europe to the sun-kissed terrains of Asia, the allure of rosehip vinegars and shrubs has transcended cultural boundaries, leaving an indelible mark on the palates of connoisseurs and enthusiasts alike. Join us as we uncover the secrets behind the creation of these exquisite elixirs, from the meticulous selection of the finest rosehips to the intricate methods of fermentation and infusion.

Learn about the nuanced balance of flavors that define each variation, and discover the innovative ways in which chefs and mixologists have woven these essences into their culinary tapestries. Whether employed as a tantalizing ingredient in a gourmet dish or as a refreshing component of a bespoke cocktail, rosehip vinegars and shrubs continue to enchant and inspire, offering a sensory escapade that is as timeless as it is contemporary.

Ancient Greek Style Rosehip Vinegar

Ancient Greek Style Rosehip Vinegar is a tribute to the rich culinary heritage of Greece, steeped in tradition and revered for its medicinal and gastronomic virtues. This exquisite vinegar embodies the essence of ancient Greek flavors, boasting a perfect balance of sweet and tart notes, complemented by a delicate floral aroma. Utilized in both culinary and wellness practices, this vinegar has its roots in the ancient Greek civilizations, where the rosehip was celebrated for its diverse health benefits and culinary versatility.

Originating from the sun-kissed landscapes of ancient Greece, this vinegar was highly valued for its therapeutic properties and was often used as a natural remedy for various ailments. The ancient Greeks believed in the rejuvenating and invigorating properties of rosehips, incorporating them into their diets and wellness regimens. With its rich history intertwined with Greek culture, this vinegar serves as a testament to the enduring legacy of the rosehip in the Mediterranean region.

Here is a simple recipe for Ancient Greek Style Rosehip Vinegar:

Ingredients:

- 2 cups fresh rosehips
- 4 cups red wine vinegar
- 1 tablespoon honey
- 1 cinnamon stick (optional)
- Sterilized glass bottle or jar

Instructions:

1. Rinse the fresh rosehips thoroughly and pat them dry.
2. Use a sharp knife to carefully remove the stems and blossom ends of the rosehips.
3. Gently crush the rosehips to release their juices and flavors.
4. In a saucepan, heat the red wine vinegar over low heat. Add the crushed rosehips, honey, and cinnamon stick, if desired.
5. Simmer the mixture for about 10-15 minutes, allowing the flavors to infuse.
6. Remove the saucepan from the heat and let the mixture cool to room temperature.
7. Strain the liquid through a fine mesh sieve or cheesecloth to remove the solid pieces.
8. Pour the strained liquid into a sterilized glass bottle or jar.
9. Seal the container and store it in a cool, dark place for at least a week to allow the flavors to develop.
10. Once the desired flavor is achieved, use the Ancient Greek Style Rosehip Vinegar to elevate salads, marinades, and various culinary creations, paying homage to the ancient Greek culinary traditions.

Ancient Egyptian Style Rosehip Vinegar

Ancient Egyptian Style Rosehip Vinegar is a nod to the storied culinary and medicinal practices of ancient Egypt, renowned for their deep reverence for the natural world and its offerings. This vinegar embodies the essence of ancient Egyptian flavors, characterized by a delicate balance of tangy and sweet nuances, coupled with a subtle floral fragrance. Embodying a cultural legacy that revered the rosehip for its therapeutic properties and culinary versatility, this vinegar pays homage to the ancient Egyptians' profound understanding of the healing power of natural ingredients.

Originating from the fertile lands along the Nile River, this vinegar reflects the historical significance of the rosehip in ancient Egyptian culture, where it was cherished for its multifaceted benefits and its integral role in ancient herbal remedies and culinary practices. With its roots intertwined in the rich tapestry of ancient Egyptian traditions, this vinegar serves as a testament to the enduring legacy of the rosehip in the ancient world.

Here is a simple recipe for Ancient Egyptian Style Rosehip Vinegar:

Ingredients:

- 2 cups fresh or dried rosehips
- 4 cups apple cider vinegar
- 1 tablespoon raw honey or date syrup
- 1 pinch of dried hibiscus petals (optional for an Egyptian twist)
- Sterilized glass bottle or jar

Instructions:

1. Thoroughly wash the fresh rosehips and remove the stems and blossom ends.
2. If using dried rosehips, rinse them in cold water to remove any impurities.
3. Gently crush the rosehips to release their essence and flavor.
4. In a saucepan, heat the apple cider vinegar over low heat. Add the crushed rosehips, raw honey or date syrup, and dried hibiscus petals, if using.
5. Allow the mixture to simmer for approximately 15-20 minutes, infusing the vinegar with the flavors of the rosehips and hibiscus.
6. Remove the saucepan from the heat and let the mixture cool to room temperature.
7. Strain the liquid through a fine mesh sieve or cheesecloth to remove any solid pieces.
8. Transfer the strained liquid into a sterilized glass bottle or jar.
9. Seal the container and store it in a cool, dark place for at least a week, allowing the flavors to meld and mature.
10. Embrace the essence of ancient Egypt by using the Ancient Egyptian Style Rosehip Vinegar to enhance dressings, marinades, and other culinary creations, celebrating the rich tapestry of flavors that defined the ancient Egyptian palate.

Ancient Roman Style Rosehip Vinegar

Ancient Roman Style Rosehip Vinegar pays homage to the culinary and wellness practices of the ancient Romans, celebrated for their refined tastes and deep appreciation for the natural world. This vinegar encapsulates the essence of ancient Roman flavors, characterized by a harmonious blend of tangy sweetness and subtle floral undertones. Rooted in the historical significance of the rosehip in ancient Roman culture, this vinegar reflects the Romans' reverence for this versatile fruit and its myriad uses in both culinary and medicinal contexts.

Hailing from the sun-drenched hills of ancient Rome, this vinegar is a testament to the Romans' sophisticated understanding of the therapeutic benefits of the rosehip. Recognized for its rejuvenating and invigorating properties, the rosehip held a significant place in ancient Roman cuisine and holistic wellness practices. Through the lens of this ancient vinegar, we are reminded of the enduring legacy of the rosehip in the rich tapestry of ancient Roman traditions.

Here is a simple recipe for Ancient Roman Style Rosehip Vinegar:

Ingredients:

- 2 cups fresh rosehips
- 4 cups white wine vinegar
- 2 tablespoons raw honey
- 1 sprig of fresh thyme (optional)
- Sterilized glass bottle or jar

Instructions:

1. Wash the fresh rosehips thoroughly, removing the stems and blossom ends.
2. Gently crush the rosehips to release their flavors and juices.
3. In a saucepan, heat the white wine vinegar over low heat. Add the crushed rosehips, raw honey, and fresh thyme, if using.
4. Let the mixture simmer for about 15-20 minutes, allowing the vinegar to infuse with the essence of the rosehips and thyme.
5. Remove the saucepan from the heat and let the mixture cool to room temperature.
6. Strain the liquid through a fine mesh sieve or cheesecloth to remove any solid pieces.
7. Transfer the strained liquid into a sterilized glass bottle or jar.
8. Seal the container and store it in a cool, dark place for at least a week, allowing the flavors to meld and mature.
9. Embrace the legacy of ancient Rome by using the Ancient Roman Style Rosehip Vinegar to elevate sauces, vinaigrettes, and other culinary creations, channeling the timeless essence of the ancient Roman palate.

Simple Medieval Style Rosehip Vinegar

Medieval Style Rosehip Vinegar is a reflection of the rich culinary traditions and herbal practices of the Middle Ages, a time when the use of natural ingredients held a significant place in the daily lives of people. This vinegar encapsulates the essence of medieval flavors, characterized by a delicate balance of tartness and subtle floral aromas. Deeply rooted in the historical significance of the rosehip during the Middle Ages, this vinegar stands as a testament to the medieval period's reverence for the therapeutic properties and culinary versatility of this cherished fruit.

Emerging from the castle kitchens and monastic gardens of medieval Europe, this vinegar embodies the essence of the rosehip as a symbol of vitality and well-being. Valued for its immune-boosting and digestive properties, the rosehip was commonly utilized in various medieval recipes and herbal remedies. By exploring the medieval style of preparing rosehip vinegar, we are transported back to a time when the healing power of natural ingredients was woven into the fabric of everyday life.

Here is a simple recipe for Medieval Style Rosehip Vinegar:

Ingredients:

- 2 cups fresh or dried rosehips
- 4 cups cider vinegar
- 2 tablespoons raw honey or brown sugar
- 1 small sprig of fresh rosemary (optional)
- Sterilized glass bottle or jar

Instructions:

1. If using fresh rosehips, rinse them thoroughly and remove any stems or blossom ends. If using dried rosehips, rinse them to remove any debris.
2. Crush the rosehips slightly to release their flavors.
3. In a saucepan, heat the cider vinegar over low heat. Add the crushed rosehips, raw honey or brown sugar, and the fresh rosemary sprig, if using.
4. Allow the mixture to simmer for approximately 20-25 minutes, infusing the vinegar with the essence of the rosehips and rosemary.
5. Remove the saucepan from the heat and let the mixture cool to room temperature.
6. Strain the liquid through a fine mesh sieve or cheesecloth to remove any solid pieces.
7. Transfer the strained liquid into a sterilized glass bottle or jar.
8. Seal the container and store it in a cool, dark place for at least a week, allowing the flavors to meld and mature.
9. Experience the essence of the medieval period by using the Medieval Style Rosehip Vinegar to enhance stews, marinades, and other culinary creations, honoring the rich tapestry of flavors that defined the medieval palate.

Complex Medieval Style Rosehip Vinegar

Ingredients:

- 4 cups fresh rosehips
- 6 cups white wine vinegar
- 2 cups honey or brown sugar
- 1 tablespoon whole cloves
- 1 tablespoon whole allspice
- 2 cinnamon sticks
- 1 small piece of ginger, peeled and sliced
- 1 vanilla bean, split lengthwise
- Sterilized glass jar or bottle with airtight lid

Instructions:

1. Begin by thoroughly cleaning the fresh rosehips, removing any stems or blossom ends. Pat them dry with a clean kitchen towel.
2. In a large saucepan, combine the white wine vinegar and honey or brown sugar over low heat. Stir gently until the sweetener dissolves completely.
3. Add the cleaned rosehips to the saucepan, along with the whole cloves, whole allspice, cinnamon sticks, sliced ginger, and split vanilla bean.
4. Allow the mixture to simmer on low heat for approximately 30-40 minutes, infusing the vinegar with the rich flavors of the rosehips and aromatic spices.
5. After simmering, remove the saucepan from the heat and let it cool to room temperature.
6. Carefully pour the cooled mixture into a sterilized glass jar or bottle, ensuring that all the rosehips and spices are transferred.
7. Seal the jar or bottle with an airtight lid and store it in a cool, dark place for at least 6-8 weeks, allowing the flavors to meld and mature.
8. After the steeping period, strain the liquid through a fine mesh sieve or cheesecloth to remove all solid ingredients, capturing the richly infused rosehip vinegar.
9. Transfer the strained vinegar back into the sterilized glass jar or bottle and seal it tightly.
10. Store the Medieval Style Rosehip Vinegar in a cool, dark place, and savor the authentic flavors of the Middle Ages by using it to elevate sauces, glazes, and other culinary creations.

This intricate process captures the essence of the medieval era, allowing you to immerse yourself in the historical culinary traditions of the Middle Ages through the intricate and nuanced flavors of this exceptional rosehip vinegar.

Three Complex Medieval Style Rosehip Vinegar Cocktails

1. Royal Rosehip Fizz:

Ingredients:

- 1 ½ oz gin
- 1 oz Complex Medieval Style Rosehip Vinegar
- ½ oz elderflower liqueur
- ½ oz fresh lemon juice
- 1 egg white
- Club soda
- Rose petals for garnish

Instructions:

1. Dry shake the gin, Complex Medieval Style Rosehip Vinegar, elderflower liqueur, fresh lemon juice, and egg white in a cocktail shaker without ice for 10-15 seconds.
2. Add ice to the shaker and shake vigorously for another 15-20 seconds.
3. Strain the mixture into a chilled highball glass over ice.
4. Top off with club soda and gently stir.
5. Garnish with fresh rose petals for an elegant and aromatic presentation.

2. Nobleman's Elixir:

Ingredients:

- 2 oz bourbon
- 1 oz Complex Medieval Style Rosehip Vinegar
- ¼ oz maple syrup
- 2 dashes of bitters
- Orange twist for garnish

Instructions:

1. In a mixing glass, combine the bourbon, Complex Medieval Style Rosehip Vinegar, maple syrup, and bitters.
2. Fill the mixing glass with ice and stir for 30 seconds to chill the mixture.
3. Strain the elixir into a chilled rocks glass over a large ice cube.
4. Express the oil from an orange twist over the drink and use it as a garnish for a citrusy aroma.

3. Castle Garden Sour:

Ingredients:

- 1 ½ oz rye whiskey
- ¾ oz Complex Medieval Style Rosehip Vinegar
- ½ oz honey syrup
- ½ oz fresh lime juice
- 1 dash of Angostura bitters
- Rosemary sprig for garnish

Instructions:

1. In a shaker, combine the rye whiskey, Complex Medieval Style Rosehip Vinegar, honey syrup, fresh lime juice, and a dash of Angostura bitters.
2. Fill the shaker with ice and shake vigorously for 15-20 seconds.
3. Strain the mixture into a chilled coupe glass.
4. Garnish with a fresh rosemary sprig for an earthy and aromatic touch. Enjoy the Castle Garden Sour, a refined and complex libation that showcases the depth and richness of the Complex Medieval Style Rosehip Vinegar, balanced with the robust flavors of rye whiskey and the subtle sweetness of honey.

Ten Shrubs with Cocktails

Welcome to a world of exquisite flavors and historical marvels! In this collection, we present a tantalizing array of shrub recipes, each showcasing the rich nuances of ancient vinegars steeped in tradition. From the mystique of Ancient Roman Style Rosehip Vinegar to the earthy warmth of Medieval Style Rosehip Vinegar, these concoctions pay homage to the culinary heritage of civilizations past.

Embrace the essence of the past as we delve into the art of crafting shrubs, marrying the robust profiles of rosehip vinegars with an array of carefully curated ingredients. Whether you seek a zesty infusion or a mellow blend, these shrub recipes are crafted to tantalize the taste buds and offer a refreshing escape into the flavors of antiquity.

Indulge in the time-honored practice of crafting shrubs as we journey through a tapestry of ancient flavors, each blend reflecting the unique character and influence of its historical origin. Let each sip be a celebration of the ingenuity and creativity that have flourished across cultures throughout the ages.

1. Rosehip-Basil Shrub

Introducing the captivating Rosehip-Basil Shrub, a harmonious blend that marries the enchanting essence of rosehips with the aromatic allure of fresh basil. With origins rooted in the historical reverence for natural ingredients, this shrub encapsulates the time-honored tradition of crafting flavorsome infusions.

Tasting Notes:
The Rosehip-Basil Shrub tantalizes the palate with a delicate balance of tartness from the rosehips and a subtle hint of herbal freshness from the basil. The amalgamation of these distinct elements creates a vibrant profile that is both invigorating and soothing.

Pairing Suggestions:
This shrub is a versatile addition to both mocktails and cocktails, adding a sophisticated twist to your favorite beverages. Pair it with sparkling water to savor its refreshing zest, or incorporate it into craft cocktails to elevate the overall flavor profile. It also complements light salads, grilled vegetables, and seafood dishes, imparting a subtle yet distinctive tang.

Experience the Rosehip-Basil Shrub as it invites you on a sensory journey, evoking the essence of bygone eras while seamlessly complementing contemporary culinary creations. Revel in the fusion of flavors and the intriguing interplay of historical significance with modern-day indulgence.

Ingredients:

- 1 cup fresh or dried rosehips
- 4 cups apple cider vinegar
- 1 cup fresh basil leaves, loosely packed
- 1 cup granulated sugar or honey (adjust to taste)
- Sterilized glass jar or bottle with airtight lid

Instructions:

1. If using fresh rosehips, thoroughly rinse them and remove any stems or blossom ends. For dried rosehips, ensure they are clean and free of impurities.
2. In a saucepan, combine the apple cider vinegar and rosehips over low heat. Let the mixture simmer for 20-25 minutes, allowing the vinegar to infuse with the essence of the rosehips.
3. Strain the mixture through a fine mesh sieve or cheesecloth to remove the rosehips, allowing the infused vinegar to cool to room temperature.
4. In a separate bowl, gently muddle the fresh basil leaves to release their oils and aroma.
5. Combine the basil with the rosehip-infused vinegar and sugar or honey in a

clean saucepan. Heat the mixture over low heat, stirring continuously until the sweetener is fully dissolved.

6. Let the mixture simmer for an additional 10-15 minutes to allow the flavors to meld.

7. Remove the saucepan from the heat and let the shrub cool to room temperature.

8. Once cooled, transfer the shrub to a sterilized glass jar or bottle, ensuring a secure seal with an airtight lid.

9. Store the Rosehip-Basil Shrub in a cool, dark place for at least 2-3 weeks, allowing the flavors to further develop and mature.

10. Give the jar or bottle a gentle shake every few days to ensure the ingredients are thoroughly combined.

11. Enjoy the Rosehip-Basil Shrub by adding a splash to sparkling water or incorporating it into creative cocktails and mocktails for a refreshing burst of flavor.

Cocktail: Basil-Rosehip Elixir

Ingredients:

- 1 ½ oz gin
- 1 oz Rosehip-Basil Shrub
- ½ oz elderflower liqueur
- ¾ oz freshly squeezed lemon juice
- ½ oz simple syrup
- Fresh basil leaves for garnish

Instructions:

1. In a cocktail shaker, combine the gin, Rosehip-Basil Shrub, elderflower liqueur, freshly squeezed lemon juice, and simple syrup.

2. Fill the shaker with ice and shake vigorously for 15-20 seconds to chill the mixture.

3. Strain the contents into a chilled coupe glass.

4. Garnish with a sprig of fresh basil leaves to add a fragrant and herbal aroma to the presentation.

5. Savor the Basil-Rosehip Elixir, allowing the intricate blend of flavors to envelop your senses, with the herbaceous notes of basil complementing the tangy sweetness of the Rosehip-Basil Shrub.

Embrace the exquisite fusion of botanical essences and the refined complexity of the Basil-Rosehip Elixir, celebrating the art of mixology with a cocktail that embodies both sophistication and depth.

2. Rosehip-Spiced Apple Shrub

The Rosehip-Spiced Apple Shrub is a captivating infusion that intertwines the delicate essence of rosehips with the comforting familiarity of spiced apple. With origins steeped in culinary heritage, this shrub offers a delightful blend of sweet and tangy flavors, embodying a harmonious balance of tradition and innovation.

Tasting Notes:
Experience the delightful interplay of the tartness from the rosehips harmonizing with the warmth of spiced apple, creating a nuanced profile that is both invigorating and comforting. The aromatic notes of cinnamon and nutmeg add a cozy depth, making each sip a journey through layers of rich, autumnal flavors.

Ingredients:

- 1 cup fresh or dried rosehips
- 4 cups apple cider vinegar
- 2 cups freshly pressed apple juice
- 1/2 teaspoon ground cinnamon
- A pinch of nutmeg
- 1 cup granulated sugar or honey (adjust to taste)
- Sterilized glass jar or bottle with airtight lid

Instructions:

1. If using fresh rosehips, thoroughly rinse them and remove any stems or blossom ends. If using dried rosehips, ensure they are clean and free of impurities.
2. In a saucepan, combine the apple cider vinegar and rosehips over low heat. Let the mixture simmer for 20-25 minutes, allowing the vinegar to infuse with the essence of the rosehips.
3. Strain the mixture through a fine mesh sieve or cheesecloth to remove the rosehips, allowing the infused vinegar to cool to room temperature.
4. In a separate bowl, combine the freshly pressed apple juice, ground cinnamon, and a pinch of nutmeg, mixing well.
5. Combine the spiced apple juice with the rosehip-infused vinegar and sugar or honey in a clean saucepan. Heat the mixture over low heat, stirring continuously until the sweetener is fully dissolved.
6. Let the mixture simmer for an additional 10-15 minutes to allow the flavors to meld.
7. Remove the saucepan from the heat and let the shrub cool to room temperature.
8. Once cooled, transfer the shrub to a sterilized glass jar or bottle, ensuring a secure seal with an airtight lid.

9. Store the Rosehip-Spiced Apple Shrub in a cool, dark place for at least 2-3 weeks, allowing the flavors to further develop and mature.
10. Give the jar or bottle a gentle shake every few days to ensure the ingredients are thoroughly combined.
11. Enjoy the Rosehip-Spiced Apple Shrub by adding a splash to sparkling water or incorporating it into creative cocktails and mocktails for a delightful blend of fruitiness and warmth.

Cocktail: Rosehip-Spiced Apple Sparkler

Ingredients:
- 2 oz vodka
- 1 oz Rosehip-Spiced Apple Shrub
- 4 oz sparkling water
- Apple slices and cinnamon sticks for garnish

Instructions:
1. Fill a cocktail shaker with ice and add the vodka and Rosehip-Spiced Apple Shrub.
2. Shake vigorously for about 15 seconds to chill the mixture.
3. Strain the contents into a chilled glass filled with ice.
4. Top with sparkling water and gently stir to combine.
5. Garnish with apple slices and a cinnamon stick for an added touch of elegance.
6. Savor the Rosehip-Spiced Apple Sparkler and relish the refreshing blend of fruity sweetness and warming spices, perfect for any occasion.

Indulge in the Rosehip-Spiced Apple Shrub as it elevates your cocktail experience, adding a layer of sophistication and depth to your favorite libations. Allow the richness of this shrub to transport you to an enchanting world of balanced flavors and timeless appeal.

3. Rosehip-Lemon Thyme Shrub Recipe

Indulge in the Rosehip-Lemon Thyme Shrub, an artful concoction that encapsulates the essence of the Mediterranean countryside, with its vibrant citrusy undertones and aromatic herbaceous notes. Embrace the time-honored tradition of crafting shrubs as this delightful blend invites you to experience the synergy of natural ingredients and culinary finesse.

Ingredients:

- 1 cup fresh or dried rosehips
- 4 cups apple cider vinegar
- 1 cup fresh lemon juice
- 3 sprigs of fresh thyme
- 1 cup granulated sugar or honey (adjust to taste)
- Sterilized glass jar or bottle with airtight lid

Instructions:

1. Rinse the rosehips thoroughly, removing any stems or blossom ends. If using dried rosehips, ensure they are clean and free of impurities.
2. In a saucepan, combine the apple cider vinegar and rosehips over low heat. Let the mixture simmer for 20-25 minutes to infuse the vinegar with the essence of the rosehips.
3. Strain the mixture through a fine mesh sieve or cheesecloth to remove the rosehips, allowing the infused vinegar to cool to room temperature.
4. In a separate bowl, combine the fresh lemon juice and thyme sprigs, gently muddling the thyme to release its aroma.
5. Mix the lemon-thyme mixture with the rosehip-infused vinegar and sugar or honey in a clean saucepan. Heat the mixture over low heat, stirring continuously until the sweetener is fully dissolved.
6. Allow the mixture to simmer for an additional 10-15 minutes to allow the flavors to meld.
7. Remove the saucepan from the heat and let the shrub cool to room temperature.
8. Once cooled, transfer the shrub to a sterilized glass jar or bottle, ensuring a secure seal with an airtight lid.
9. Store the Rosehip-Lemon Thyme Shrub in a cool, dark place for at least 2-3 weeks to allow the flavors to mature.

Tasting Notes:
The Rosehip-Lemon Thyme Shrub boasts a delightful fusion of tangy citrus notes from the lemon, complemented by the subtle herbal essence of fresh thyme. The gentle tartness of the rosehips enhances the overall complexity, creating a well-rounded and refreshing flavor profile.

Cocktail: Rosehip-Thyme Sparkler

Ingredients:

- 1 ½ oz vodka
- 1 oz Rosehip-Lemon Thyme Shrub
- 3 oz sparkling water
- Fresh thyme and lemon peel for garnish

Instructions:

1. Fill a cocktail shaker with ice and add the vodka and Rosehip-Lemon Thyme Shrub.
2. Shake vigorously for about 15 seconds to chill the mixture.
3. Strain the contents into a chilled glass filled with ice.
4. Top with sparkling water and gently stir to combine.
5. Garnish with a sprig of fresh thyme and a twist of lemon peel for an added visual appeal.
6. Savor the Rosehip-Thyme Sparkler, a tantalizing blend of herbal sophistication and citrusy effervescence, perfect for any occasion.

4. Rosehip-Ginger Shrub

Embrace the alluring fusion of tart rosehips and zesty ginger in the Rosehip-Ginger Shrub, a testament to the art of crafting flavorful infusions. Revel in the juxtaposition of vibrant tanginess and subtle heat, as this shrub evokes a sense of culinary adventure and cultural richness.

Ingredients:

- 1 cup fresh or dried rosehips
- 4 cups apple cider vinegar
- 1 cup granulated sugar or honey (adjust to taste)
- 1 large ginger root, peeled and thinly sliced
- Sterilized glass jar or bottle with airtight lid

Instructions:

1. Thoroughly clean the rosehips, removing any stems or blossom ends. If using dried rosehips, ensure they are free of impurities.
2. In a saucepan, combine the apple cider vinegar and rosehips over low heat. Simmer the mixture for 20-25 minutes, allowing the vinegar to infuse with the essence of the rosehips.
3. Strain the mixture through a fine mesh sieve or cheesecloth, removing the rosehips and allowing the infused vinegar to cool to room temperature.
4. In a separate saucepan, combine the ginger slices with the sugar or honey, heating over low heat until the sweetener dissolves and the ginger infuses the mixture.
5. Combine the ginger-infused sweetener with the rosehip-infused vinegar, stirring gently to ensure the flavors meld together.
6. Let the mixture cool to room temperature before transferring it to a sterilized glass jar or bottle with an airtight lid.
7. Store the Rosehip-Ginger Shrub in a cool, dark place for at least 2-3 weeks, allowing the flavors to fully develop and mature.

Tasting Notes:
The Rosehip-Ginger Shrub boasts a captivating fusion of the tangy essence of rosehips, complemented by the warm, spicy notes of ginger. This combination creates a dynamic and invigorating flavor profile that is both refreshing and comforting.

Cocktail: Ginger-Rosehip Mule

Ingredients:

- 2 oz vodka
- 1 oz Rosehip-Ginger Shrub
- 4 oz ginger beer
- Squeeze of fresh lime juice
- Rosemary sprig and crystallized ginger for garnish

Instructions:

1. Fill a copper mug with ice and pour in the vodka and Rosehip-Ginger Shrub.
2. Add a squeeze of fresh lime juice and stir gently to combine.
3. Top with ginger beer and give the mixture a quick stir.
4. Garnish with a sprig of fresh rosemary and a piece of crystallized ginger for an aromatic and visually appealing finish.
5. Enjoy the Ginger-Rosehip Mule, an invigorating cocktail that celebrates the spirited union of zesty ginger, tangy rosehips, and the delightful warmth of vodka, creating a refreshing and uniquely nuanced libation.

5. Rosehip-Orange Cardamom Shrub Recipe

Embark on a sensory journey with the Rosehip-Orange Cardamom Shrub, a sensory delight that artfully balances the bright zest of oranges with the comforting allure of cardamom, all anchored by the subtle tang of rosehips. Revel in the fusion of cultural influences and natural ingredients that define this exquisite creation.

Ingredients:

- 1 cup fresh or dried rosehips
- 4 cups apple cider vinegar
- 1 cup granulated sugar or honey (adjust to taste)
- Zest of 2 oranges
- 1 tablespoon whole cardamom pods
- Sterilized glass jar or bottle with airtight lid

Instructions:

1. Rinse the rosehips thoroughly, removing any stems or blossom ends. If using dried rosehips, ensure they are clean and free of impurities.
2. In a saucepan, combine the apple cider vinegar and rosehips over low heat. Let the mixture simmer for 20-25 minutes to infuse the vinegar with the essence of the rosehips.
3. Strain the mixture through a fine mesh sieve or cheesecloth to remove the rosehips, allowing the infused vinegar to cool to room temperature.
4. In a separate bowl, combine the orange zest and cardamom pods, lightly crushing the cardamom to release its aroma.
5. Mix the orange-cardamom mixture with the rosehip-infused vinegar and sugar or honey in a clean saucepan. Heat the mixture over low heat, stirring continuously until the sweetener is fully dissolved.
6. Allow the mixture to simmer for an additional 10-15 minutes to allow the flavors to meld.
7. Remove the saucepan from the heat and let the shrub cool to room temperature.
8. Once cooled, transfer the shrub to a sterilized glass jar or bottle, ensuring a secure seal with an airtight lid.
9. Store the Rosehip-Orange Cardamom Shrub in a cool, dark place for at least 2-3 weeks to allow the flavors to mature.

Tasting Notes:
The Rosehip-Orange Cardamom Shrub tantalizes the taste buds with a vibrant medley of tangy orange zest, harmoniously infused with the warm, aromatic essence of cardamom. The delicate tartness of the rosehips serves to enhance the complexity of this shrub, resulting in a well-rounded and invigorating flavor experience.

Cocktail: Cardamom-Orange Rosehip Fizz

Ingredients:

- 1 ½ oz dark rum
- 1 oz Rosehip-Orange Cardamom Shrub
- 3 oz club soda
- Orange slices and crushed cardamom for garnish

Instructions:

1. Fill a highball glass with ice and pour in the dark rum and Rosehip-Orange Cardamom Shrub.
2. Stir gently to combine the ingredients.
3. Top with club soda and give it a quick stir.
4. Garnish with a slice of orange and a sprinkle of crushed cardamom for an aromatic and visually appealing finish.
5. Savor the Cardamom-Orange Rosehip Fizz, a refreshing cocktail that pays homage to the aromatic marriage of orange and cardamom, elevated by the nuanced complexity of the Rosehip-Orange Cardamom Shrub.

6. Rosehip-Pomegranate Rosemary Shrub

Immerse yourself in the opulence of the Rosehip-Pomegranate Rosemary Shrub, an intricate fusion of the tangy essence of rosehips, the luscious sweetness of pomegranate, and the fragrant allure of fresh rosemary, accentuated by a harmonious blend of warming spices and a subtle floral undertone. Delight in the layers of multifaceted flavors that weave together to create an unforgettable drinking experience reminiscent of a lavish royal banquet.

Ingredients:

- 3 cups fresh or dried rosehips
- 3 cups fresh pomegranate arils
- 5 cups apple cider vinegar
- 2 ½ cups granulated sugar or honey (adjust to taste)
- 5-6 sprigs of fresh rosemary
- 1 tablespoon whole black peppercorns
- 1 tablespoon whole cloves
- 1 teaspoon cardamom pods
- 1 teaspoon coriander seeds
- Sterilized glass jar or bottle with airtight lid

Instructions:

1. Thoroughly clean the rosehips, ensuring they are free of any impurities. If using dried rosehips, ensure they are well-cleaned.
2. In a large saucepan, combine the apple cider vinegar, rosehips, pomegranate arils, fresh rosemary sprigs, black peppercorns, cloves, cardamom pods, and coriander seeds over low heat. Let the mixture simmer for 35-40 minutes to infuse the vinegar with the rich and complex flavors.
3. Strain the mixture through a fine mesh sieve or cheesecloth, ensuring all solid ingredients are removed, and allow the infused vinegar to cool to room temperature.
4. In a separate bowl, combine the infused vinegar with the granulated sugar or honey, stirring until the sweetener is fully dissolved.
5. Let the mixture simmer for an additional 25-30 minutes to meld the intricate flavors and create depth.
6. Remove the saucepan from the heat and let the shrub cool to room temperature.
7. Once cooled, transfer the shrub to a sterilized glass jar or bottle, ensuring a secure seal with an airtight lid.
8. Store the Elaborated Rosehip-Pomegranate Rosemary Shrub in a cool, dark place for at least 5-6 weeks to allow the flavors to harmonize and develop into a sumptuous elixir.

Tasting Notes:

The Elaborated Rosehip-Pomegranate Rosemary Shrub delivers a symphony of flavors that intricately interlace the tartness of rosehips, the luscious sweetness of pomegranate, the aromatic allure of rosemary, and the complex medley of warming spices, offering a regal and sophisticated shrub that captivates the palate with its depth and opulence.

Cocktail: Regal Pomegranate Rosemary Elixir

Ingredients:

- 2 oz aged rum
- 1 ½ oz Elaborated Rosehip-Pomegranate Rosemary Shrub
- ¾ oz amaro
- ½ oz fresh lime juice
- ½ oz pomegranate molasses
- 2 dashes aromatic bitters
- Pomegranate seeds and a rosemary sprig for garnish

Instructions:

1. In a mixing glass, combine the aged rum, Elaborated Rosehip-Pomegranate Rosemary Shrub, amaro, fresh lime juice, pomegranate molasses, and aromatic bitters.
2. Fill the mixing glass with ice and stir for 30-40 seconds to marry the flavors.
3. Strain the elixir into a chilled coupe glass.
4. Garnish with a sprinkle of pomegranate seeds and a rosemary sprig for a majestic presentation.
5. Savor the Regal Pomegranate Rosemary Elixir, an indulgent and refined libation that pays homage to the intricate fusion of pomegranate, rosemary, and the intricate nuances of the Elaborated Rosehip-Pomegranate Rosemary Shrub, offering an unparalleled drinking experience steeped in grandeur and sophistication.

7. Rosehip-Cranberry Sage Shrub Recipe

Delight in the Rosehip-Cranberry Sage Shrub, a testament to the art of crafting complex yet balanced flavor combinations. This exquisite shrub embodies the essence of autumnal richness, blending the vibrant hues and flavors of cranberries and rosehips with the aromatic allure of fresh sage.

Ingredients:

- 1 cup fresh or dried rosehips
- 1 cup fresh or frozen cranberries
- 4 cups apple cider vinegar
- 1 cup granulated sugar or honey (adjust to taste)
- 6-8 fresh sage leaves
- Sterilized glass jar or bottle with airtight lid

Instructions:

1. Rinse the rosehips thoroughly, removing any stems or blossom ends. If using dried rosehips, ensure they are clean and free of impurities.
2. In a saucepan, combine the apple cider vinegar, rosehips, and cranberries over low heat. Let the mixture simmer for 20-25 minutes to infuse the vinegar with the essence of the ingredients.
3. Strain the mixture through a fine mesh sieve or cheesecloth to remove the rosehips and cranberries, allowing the infused vinegar to cool to room temperature.
4. In a separate bowl, combine the fresh sage leaves with the sugar or honey, gently bruising the sage to release its aroma.
5. Mix the sage-infused sweetener with the rosehip-cranberry-infused vinegar in a clean saucepan. Heat the mixture over low heat, stirring continuously until the sweetener is fully dissolved.
6. Allow the mixture to simmer for an additional 10-15 minutes to allow the flavors to meld.
7. Remove the saucepan from the heat and let the shrub cool to room temperature.
8. Once cooled, transfer the shrub to a sterilized glass jar or bottle, ensuring a secure seal with an airtight lid.
9. Store the Rosehip-Cranberry Sage Shrub in a cool, dark place for at least 2-3 weeks to allow the flavors to mature.

Tasting Notes:
The Rosehip-Cranberry Sage Shrub entices with a harmonious blend of tangy cranberries and the delicate tartness of rosehips, beautifully complemented by the earthy, aromatic essence of fresh sage. This medley creates a nuanced flavor profile that is simultaneously bright, herbaceous, and delightfully refreshing.

Cocktail: Cranberry-Sage Rosehip Smash

Ingredients:

- 2 oz bourbon
- 1 ½ oz Rosehip-Cranberry Sage Shrub
- ½ oz freshly squeezed lemon juice
- Fresh cranberries and sage leaves for garnish

Instructions:

1. In a cocktail shaker, combine the bourbon, Rosehip-Cranberry Sage Shrub, and lemon juice.
2. Add ice and shake vigorously for 15-20 seconds to chill the mixture.
3. Strain the contents into a rocks glass filled with ice.
4. Garnish with a skewer of fresh cranberries and a sprig of sage for an elegant and seasonal presentation.
5. Savor the Cranberry-Sage Rosehip Smash, a sophisticated libation that embodies the rich flavors of autumn, harmonizing the robust essence of bourbon with the vibrant tang of cranberries and the subtle herbal notes of sage.

8. Rosehip-Blackberry Mint Shrub

Indulge in the Rosehip-Blackberry Mint Shrub, a testament to the art of crafting well-balanced and invigorating flavor combinations. Experience the lively fusion of luscious blackberries and tart rosehips, enhanced by the cooling essence of mint, offering a sensory journey that is both revitalizing and delightful.

Ingredients:

- 1 cup fresh or dried rosehips
- 1 cup fresh or frozen blackberries
- 4 cups apple cider vinegar
- 1 cup granulated sugar or honey (adjust to taste)
- 10-12 fresh mint leaves
- Sterilized glass jar or bottle with airtight lid

Instructions:

1. Thoroughly clean the rosehips, removing any stems or blossom ends. If using dried rosehips, ensure they are clean and free of impurities.
2. In a saucepan, combine the apple cider vinegar, rosehips, and blackberries over low heat. Let the mixture simmer for 20-25 minutes to infuse the vinegar with the essence of the ingredients.
3. Strain the mixture through a fine mesh sieve or cheesecloth to remove the rosehips and blackberries, allowing the infused vinegar to cool to room temperature.
4. In a separate bowl, combine the fresh mint leaves with the sugar or honey, gently bruising the mint to release its aroma.
5. Mix the mint-infused sweetener with the rosehip-blackberry-infused vinegar in a clean saucepan. Heat the mixture over low heat, stirring continuously until the sweetener is fully dissolved.
6. Allow the mixture to simmer for an additional 10-15 minutes to allow the flavors to meld.
7. Remove the saucepan from the heat and let the shrub cool to room temperature.
8. Once cooled, transfer the shrub to a sterilized glass jar or bottle, ensuring a secure seal with an airtight lid.
9. Store the Rosehip-Blackberry Mint Shrub in a cool, dark place for at least 2-3 weeks to allow the flavors to fully develop.

Tasting Notes:
The Rosehip-Blackberry Mint Shrub captivates with a vibrant blend of tangy blackberries and the delicate tartness of rosehips, accentuated by the invigorating coolness of fresh mint. This medley creates a refreshing and harmonious flavor profile that is both bright and soothing.

Cocktail: Blackberry-Mint Rosehip Refresher

Ingredients:

- 2 oz silver rum
- 1 ½ oz Rosehip-Blackberry Mint Shrub
- 3-4 oz club soda
- Fresh blackberries and mint sprig for garnish

Instructions:

1. Fill a Collins glass with ice and pour in the silver rum and Rosehip-Blackberry Mint Shrub.
2. Stir gently to combine the ingredients.
3. Top with club soda and give it a quick stir.
4. Garnish with a few fresh blackberries and a sprig of mint for an elegant and visually appealing finish.
5. Savor the Blackberry-Mint Rosehip Refresher, a revitalizing libation that celebrates the vibrant union of blackberries, mint, and the nuanced complexity of the Rosehip-Blackberry Mint Shrub, offering a refreshing and layered drinking experience.
   - Infuse 1 cup of Ancient Egyptian Style Rosehip Vinegar with 1 cup of muddled blackberries and 1/4 cup of fresh mint leaves.

9. Rosehip-Plum Clove Shrub Recipe

Delight in the Rosehip-Plum Clove Shrub, an embodiment of the art of combining rich, seasonal flavors. Experience the dynamic harmony of tart rosehips, succulent plums, and the gentle warmth of cloves, evoking a sense of culinary nostalgia and indulgence.

Ingredients:

- 1 cup fresh or dried rosehips
- 2 cups ripe plums, pitted and chopped
- 4 cups apple cider vinegar
- 1 cup granulated sugar or honey (adjust to taste)
- 8-10 whole cloves
- Sterilized glass jar or bottle with airtight lid

Instructions:

1. Rinse the rosehips thoroughly, removing any stems or blossom ends. If using dried rosehips, ensure they are clean and free of impurities.
2. In a saucepan, combine the apple cider vinegar, rosehips, and chopped plums over low heat. Let the mixture simmer for 20-25 minutes to infuse the vinegar with the essence of the ingredients.
3. Strain the mixture through a fine mesh sieve or cheesecloth to remove the rosehips and plums, allowing the infused vinegar to cool to room temperature.
4. In a separate bowl, combine the whole cloves with the sugar or honey, gently crushing the cloves to release their aroma.
5. Mix the clove-infused sweetener with the rosehip-plum-infused vinegar in a clean saucepan. Heat the mixture over low heat, stirring continuously until the sweetener is fully dissolved.
6. Allow the mixture to simmer for an additional 10-15 minutes to allow the flavors to meld.
7. Remove the saucepan from the heat and let the shrub cool to room temperature.
8. Once cooled, transfer the shrub to a sterilized glass jar or bottle, ensuring a secure seal with an airtight lid.
9. Store the Rosehip-Plum Clove Shrub in a cool, dark place for at least 2-3 weeks to allow the flavors to fully develop.

Tasting Notes:
The Rosehip-Plum Clove Shrub presents a delightful fusion of the tangy essence of rosehips, the luscious sweetness of ripe plums, and the warm, aromatic hints of cloves. This medley creates a complex and inviting flavor profile that is both comforting and exhilarating.

Cocktail: Spiced Rosehip-Plum Clove Elixir

Ingredients:

- 1 ½ oz aged rum
- 1 oz Rosehip-Plum Clove Shrub
- ½ oz fresh lemon juice
- ½ oz honey or simple syrup
- 1 egg white
- Dash of aromatic bitters
- Freshly grated nutmeg for garnish

Instructions:

1. In a cocktail shaker, combine the aged rum, Rosehip-Plum Clove Shrub, fresh lemon juice, honey or simple syrup, and egg white.
2. Dry shake (without ice) vigorously for 10-15 seconds to emulsify the egg white.
3. Add ice to the shaker and shake again until well chilled.
4. Strain the mixture into a chilled coupe glass.
5. Add a dash of aromatic bitters on top of the foam.
6. Garnish with a sprinkle of freshly grated nutmeg for an aromatic finish.
7. Enjoy the Spiced Rosehip-Plum Clove Elixir, an exquisite cocktail that seamlessly melds the rich, spiced flavors of the Rosehip-Plum Clove Shrub with the velvety texture of the egg white, offering a sophisticated and indulgent drinking experience.

10. An Elevated Rosehip-Fig Vanilla Shrub Recipe

To end with, here is a complex and intricate Rosehip-Fig Vanilla Shrub recipe featuring a nuanced and intricate taste profile, capturing the rich essence of the varied ingredients, resulting in a truly sophisticated and remarkable shrub.

Ingredients:

- 1 ½ cups fresh or dried rosehips
- 3 cups fresh figs, quartered
- 5 cups apple cider vinegar
- 2 cups granulated sugar or honey (adjust to taste)
- 2 vanilla beans, split lengthwise
- 1 teaspoon whole black peppercorns
- 1 teaspoon whole allspice berries
- 1 small piece of ginger, sliced
- 1 small piece of orange peel
- Sterilized glass jar or bottle with airtight lid

Instructions:

1. Begin by thoroughly cleaning the rosehips, ensuring they are free of any impurities. If using dried rosehips, make sure they are well-cleaned.
2. In a large saucepan, combine the apple cider vinegar, rosehips, quartered figs, black peppercorns, allspice berries, sliced ginger, and orange peel over low heat. Let the mixture simmer for 30-35 minutes to infuse the vinegar with the complex flavors.
3. Strain the mixture through a fine mesh sieve or cheesecloth, ensuring all solid ingredients are removed, and allow the infused vinegar to cool to room temperature.
4. In a separate bowl, combine the split vanilla beans with the sugar or honey, scraping the seeds from the beans to infuse the sweetener with their essence.
5. Mix the vanilla-infused sweetener with the rosehip-fig-infused vinegar in a clean saucepan. Heat the mixture over low heat, stirring continuously until the sweetener is fully dissolved.
6. Allow the mixture to simmer for an additional 15-20 minutes to deepen the flavors and complexities.
7. Remove the saucepan from the heat and let the shrub cool to room temperature.
8. Once cooled, transfer the shrub to a sterilized glass jar or bottle, ensuring a secure seal with an airtight lid.
9. Store the Elevated Rosehip-Fig Vanilla Shrub in a cool, dark place for at least 4-6 weeks to allow the intricate flavors to meld and develop.

Tasting Notes:
The Elevated Rosehip-Fig Vanilla Shrub presents an unparalleled symphony of flavors, boasting the harmonious fusion of tart rosehips, succulent figs, and the intricate blend of vanilla, black peppercorns, allspice, ginger, and citrus. This complexity creates an exquisite and refined shrub that delights the palate with its depth and sophistication.

Cocktail: Opulent Fig-Vanilla Elixir

Ingredients:

2 oz cognac
1 ½ oz Rosehip-Fig Vanilla Shrub
½ oz sweet vermouth
½ oz fresh lemon juice
1 barspoon fig preserves
1 dash aromatic bitters
Fresh fig slices and a vanilla pod for garnish

Instructions:

1. In a mixing glass, combine the cognac, Rosehip-Fig Vanilla Shrub, sweet vermouth, fresh lemon juice, fig preserves, and a dash of aromatic bitters.
2. Fill the mixing glass with ice and stir vigorously for 20-30 seconds to chill the mixture.
3. Strain the elixir into a chilled coupe glass.
4. Garnish with a couple of fresh fig slices and a split vanilla pod for an alluring presentation.
4. Sip the Opulent Fig-Vanilla Elixir, a luxurious libation that embodies the intricate fusion of figs, vanilla, and the multifaceted nuances of the Elevated Rosehip-Fig Vanilla Shrub, offering an unparalleled drinking experience steeped in refinement and grandeur.

Shrub Mocktails

Sparkling Rosehip-Pomegranate Spritz

Ingredients:

2 oz Rosehip-Pomegranate Rosemary Shrub
3 oz sparkling water
1 oz fresh lemon juice
1 tsp honey or agave syrup
Pomegranate seeds and rosemary sprig for garnish

Instructions:

1. In a shaker, combine the Rosehip-Pomegranate Rosemary Shrub, sparkling water, fresh lemon juice, and honey or agave syrup. Shake well.
2. Strain the mixture into a chilled highball glass over ice.
3. Top with a splash of sparkling water.
4. Garnish with a few pomegranate seeds and a fresh rosemary sprig for an elegant touch.

Rosehip-Pomegranate Iced Tea Refresher

Ingredients:

2 oz Rosehip-Pomegranate Rosemary Shrub
4 oz chilled black tea
1 oz fresh orange juice
Fresh mint leaves for garnish

Instructions:

1. In a shaker, combine the Rosehip-Pomegranate Rosemary Shrub, chilled black tea, and fresh orange juice. Shake gently.
2. Strain the mixture into a tall glass filled with ice.
3. Stir lightly.
4. Garnish with a few fresh mint leaves for a revitalizing and cooling touch.

Plum-Clove Sparkling Refresher

Ingredients:

- 2 oz Rosehip-Plum Clove Shrub
- 4 oz sparkling water
- 1 oz fresh lime juice
- Fresh plum slices for garnish

Instructions:

1. In a shaker, combine the Rosehip-Plum Clove Shrub, sparkling water, and fresh lime juice. Shake gently.
2. Strain the mixture into a highball glass filled with ice.
3. Top with a splash of sparkling water.
4. Garnish with fresh plum slices for a visually appealing and invigorating mocktail experience.

Cardamom-Orange Fizz Delight

Ingredients:

- 2 oz Rosehip-Orange Cardamom Shrub
- 4 oz ginger ale
- 1 oz fresh lemon juice
- Fresh orange slices for garnish

Instructions:

1. In a shaker, combine the Rosehip-Orange Cardamom Shrub, ginger ale, and fresh lemon juice. Shake well.
2. Strain the mixture into a tall glass filled with ice.
3. Top with a splash of ginger ale.
4. Garnish with fresh orange slices for a vibrant and refreshing mocktail experience.

Orange-Cardamom Sunrise Spritzer

Ingredients:

- 2 oz Rosehip-Orange Cardamom Shrub
- 4 oz sparkling water
- 1 oz fresh grapefruit juice
- Fresh cardamom pods for garnish

Instructions:

1. In a mixing glass, combine the Rosehip-Orange Cardamom Shrub, sparkling water, and fresh grapefruit juice. Stir gently.
2. Strain the mixture into a chilled highball glass over ice.
3. Garnish with a couple of fresh cardamom pods for a sophisticated and aromatic finish.

Plum-Clove Citrus Zest

Ingredients:

- 2 oz Rosehip-Plum Clove Shrub
- 4 oz chilled lemon-lime soda
- 1 oz fresh orange juice
- Fresh cloves for garnish

Instructions:

1. In a mixing glass, combine the Rosehip-Plum Clove Shrub, chilled lemon-lime soda, and fresh orange juice. Stir gently.
2. Strain the mixture into a chilled Collins glass filled with ice.
3. Garnish with a couple of fresh cloves for an aromatic and spirited touch.

Final Word on Rosehip Beverages

Incorporating rosehips, rosehip vinegars, and shrubs into cocktails, drinks, and mocktails adds a layer of sophistication and depth, elevating the overall drinking experience. The unique tartness and delicate floral notes of rosehips infuse these libations with a nuanced and refreshing character, making them stand out on any menu.

Whether creating classic cocktails with a modern twist or experimenting with historically-influenced rosehip venegars, the versatility of rosehip-based ingredients allows for a diverse range of flavors and textures. From vibrant spritzers to complex infusions, the addition of rosehips and their derived products brings an element of elegance and artistry to any beverage offering.

Furthermore, the incorporation of rosehip vinegars and shrubs in mixology introduces a dynamic interplay of sweet and tangy profiles, enhancing the overall balance and complexity of the drinks. These vinegars and shrubs, with their rich historical significance and diverse culinary applications, offer a timeless and innovative approach to crafting beverages that cater to a wide array of palates and preferences.

Ultimately, the use of rosehips and their derived products in cocktail culture presents an opportunity to create captivating and memorable drinking experiences that entice the senses and invite exploration. Whether used in traditional or avant-garde concoctions, the incorporation of rosehips and their derived elements provides a delightful journey through the rich and vibrant world of mixology.

www.ingramcontent.com/pod-product-compliance
Lightning Source LLC
Chambersburg PA
CBHW042316120626
46547CB00022B/2265